where

where no birds sing

Tales of the Supernatural in Aotearoa

Grant Shanks
with
Tahu Potiki

SHOAL BAY PRESS

First published in 1998 by
Shoal Bay Press Ltd
Box 17-661, Christchurch

Copyright © 1998 Grant Shanks

ISBN 0 908704 81 X

All rights reserved. No part of this publication may be reproduced, stored in a retrieval system or transmitted in any form by any means electronic, mechanical, photocopying, recording or otherwise, without prior permission from the publisher.

Cover design by Karl Fountaine

Printed by Rainbow Print Ltd, Christchurch

Contents

	Foreword	7
	Introduction	9
1.	The Hunter	15
2.	The House that Jack Built	18
3.	Letting Go	24
4.	Where No Birds Sing	28
5.	The Walkers	34
6.	The Right Way and the Wrong Way	39
7.	The Laying on of Hands	43
8.	The Patu	50
9.	The Cave	53
10.	The Old Lady	59
11	People Who See	61
12.	The Smell of Death	63
13.	Distant Fires	67
14	The Uninvited	74
15.	The Power of Pounamu	78
16.	The Spirit of the Ship	84
17.	The Woman in the Chair	90
18.	The Sand Dog	94
19.	No Photographs, Please	97
20.	Taniwha Tarn	100
21.	The Unhappy Tiki	104
22.	The Lady of the Lake	107
23.	Granddad's Tobacco Tin	112
24.	Waka in the Mist	117
25.	Who's Sleeping in My Bed?	122
26.	Sanctuary Tree	125
27.	Ghosts of the Living	130
28.	Home Sweet Home	132
29.	The Dead Place	137

30.	The Walking Stick	140
31	The Waterfall	142
32.	Gerald's Road	146
33.	The God Eel	149
34.	Des and the Dogs	155
35.	The Old House	159
36.	Rest in Peace	164
37.	Fire on the River	169
38.	Poker Hand	173

Foreword

My forebears, like those of many New Zealanders, came from Europe. They in turn were descended from Celts and Vikings, ancient warrior races rich in tradition, legend and superstition.

When my ancestors left Europe they left a great part of themselves behind. They left the ghosts of their past, my past, on the moors, on the grey northern seas, and in the rocks of the countryside and the stones of the old cities. Ghosts, it seems, don't travel well.

Arriving in New Zealand, these immigrants stepped ashore to find themselves in a land peopled by a race very different from what they had known. The way of life of the Maori – their culture, traditions, language and history – were totally alien to the newcomers.

The failure of the various peoples of New Zealand to understand and appreciate their respective differences is in evidence all around us today. The repercussions of this from the earliest days are a part of our heritage and are a burden we must carry.

However, this book is not about the politics of race. It is about the encounters of Pakeha with the ghosts of Maoridom. When we sailed away from our own ghosts and came to this new land, we were met by a people with a culture that revolved around spirituality and superstition. A culture in which superstition and the ghosts of the past were a part of everyday life.

Unfortunately Pakeha have been slow to acknowledge the ghosts of the Maori, and the power and significance that they have not only for the Maori people, but for all who live in this country.

This book is collection of stories told to me over a period of some 20 years by a great variety of New Zealanders – some Pakeha, some Maori, some a bit of both. In each case I have no reason to doubt their word.

Many of those who volunteered their tales are people who live and work in the bush. They are hardworking pragmatic people not given to flights of fancy. Some told me their tales in a matter-of-fact way, not really caring if I believed them or not. Others whispered their stories to me, voices low so others would not overhear.

Individual names, tribal names and some locations have been changed in these stories for obvious reasons. I have made no attempt to analyse the events that took place. The tales are as they were told to me.

Not all the tales in this collection involve Maori spirits. Pakeha in New

Zealand have been busy growing a fine crop of ghosts as well. True or false, it matters not at all. Enjoy a 'different' look at our country.

I wish to thank my friend Tahu Potiki, director of Maori Studies at the Christchurch Polytechnic, for his help and guidance in bringing this collection to print.

Grant Shanks

Introduction

In pre-European New Zealand there was no part of Maori life untouched by religion. Beliefs centred on god and ancestor worship, and a complicated set of relationships with all things in the known universe. These relationships (whakapapa) extended from the world of the living to the world of the dead; from the past into the future. There was very little distinction between gods, ancestors and man and this posed problems for a people who worshipped that which was divine.

Mana and Tapu

The proximity of the heavenly to the earthly is probably best symbolised in the concepts of mana and tapu. The gods were powerful because of mana and it was this power that made them and their actions tapu. The most tapu area in ancient times was the altar or tuaha. This was where tohunga (priests) communicated directly with the gods.

Each god had a domain of influence and people and places were dedicated to that god. A reciprocal relationship was established between the people and the god or atua. Ritual respect was paid by the people and the atua gave protection and guidance in return. Failure to follow the ritual could result in serious repercussions.

Tapu could be encountered in a residual form due to an ancient event. It could be manifest within an individual as an inherited condition, or it could be associated directly with the activities of the gods. The death of an ancestor or an event associated with a particular ancestor that could be tied to a certain locality would be enough to render that area tapu.

Tangaroa was the god of the sea and his mana could control all within it. This meant that most activities associated with the ocean required karakia or prayers to Tangaroa. Other gods, of course, had different domains of influence, and each required ritual and prayer to maintain the harmonious relationship between the people and their god.

Tapu and its potential effects required constant attention in ritual activity and prayer.

The Bones of the Dead

Traditional Maori dealt with their dead in a multitude of ways and different iwi and hapu had different death rituals and practices. Some would bury their dead facing the east, some facing north. Many still rest in secret burial caves on cliff faces and mountain tops. Some were cremated, while others were left sitting on dunes, waiting for the wind to cover them with a blanket of sand.

As is common with all peoples, the Maori buried their dead with ceremonial clothing and personal taonga or treasures. The areas associated with laying our dead to rest were and still are tapu.

It was the most grievous of insults to disturb the bones of the dead. An enemy tribe would often dig up the body of a past victim and fashion koauau (flutes) from the bones. Fish hooks were also made and used on fishing expeditions. To add insult to injury, the fishermen would then send the fish as a gift to the iwi or whanau of their victim.

Old people who were trained in the ways of the dead were not frightened to deal with bones. The act of hahu was a common practice in many tribes. After the body had mostly decomposed, the remains were gathered together and ritually prepared for sacred storage in an ornamental box or in a cave.

People appointed to care for the dead are chosen for a reason and there are often elaborate rituals to follow before bones, or koiwi, can be exhumed. Historically, a failure to observe such ritual would lead to personal misfortune.

The Spirituality of Water

Water, to the Maori, as to many other cultures, is associated with purity and life. It is considered by some the lifeblood of the Earth Mother, and as such is a mauri of the land. Water was utilised in many rituals, particularly cleansing ceremonies and baptisms.

Sacred water areas were set aside for specific rituals such as the dedication of a child to an atua or kaitiaki (guardians), while other areas were used as burial sites for certain chiefly families.

Water is also associated with divination and prophecy. The tribal tohunga would dig a small pool and study the signs made by the ripples and the reflections, predicting the fortunes of the people as they entered into battle or began a hazardous journey. Sites reserved for this purpose were very tapu and access was limited to priests and for ceremonial purposes.

Any act of misfortune either in or close to water could render the water area tapu. A rahui or period of restriction was then established. If the event was particularly powerful or the rahui was violated, the tapu and its effects could last for many years.

INTRODUCTION

Water was also the abode of taniwha and kaitiaki. Many rivers, pools and springs are associated with ancestor or god guardians. Though it may seem a little difficult to understand in modern times, many families had special protecting spirits that manifested themselves as water creatures. Although they may appear as an eel one day and as a dolphin the next, in reality they were a guardian ancestor.

While one whanau may treat the eel as a special pet, feeding it, talking to and holding counsel with it as a protector of the interests of that particular whanau, a neighbouring whanau must treat the creature warily.

Christianity and Change
While the ancient Maori religion was strong, the European missionaries brought with them a new faith, a faith powerful enough to cause the Maori to abandon their religion. Within a decade the institutional pillars of Maori religion had been destroyed and a Christian church had been built in its place.

The old beliefs and mana of the gods had seemingly disappeared, but deep down, many Maori were not yet completely convinced that Christianity was the way, and that their old religion should be abandoned. Things happened after the initial flirtation with the Christian church that caused many to look back at their past for the solutions to their problems.

In the past, ancestors had dedicated many places to the gods, creating restricted sacred areas that could not be violated. Knowledge regarding these areas was traditionally preserved within the schools of learning and the religious rites of the old people. When this hereditary chain of knowledge was broken, the protocols went unobserved and the people became ill. The elders believed the sickness was because tapu had been violated. With this in mind, they once again turned to their old priests, the tohunga.

The Role of Tohunga
On the whole, the powerful tohunga straddled two worlds. They had quickly learned the modern Christian teachings as well as having retained the knowledge of their ancestors. They visited the villages and held counsel with the elders and leaders in each community, who identified all the wahi tapu, or sacred areas of that particular hapu or sub-tribe. The sacred areas could include a burial site, an ancient place of prayer or the remnants of an old village.

In his diaries, my great-grandfather recalls the visit of one particular tohunga who had been invited to his home village. There had been much illness and it was decided that the old tapu must be cleared before wellness could be restored to the people. He describes travelling as a party to the wahi tapu and lining up behind the old man in single file as he slowly made his way onto sacred ground, praying all the way.

This particular spot had been dedicated to an important god, Kahukura, and as they moved further onto the land he appeared before them as if he were a man. The tohunga and Kahukura locked bodies in a physical struggle, although the real battle was taking place at a spiritual level. Eventually there was relief as the god disappeared and the old man was thrown high into the air, falling to the ground lifeless.

After about 30 minutes he recovered fully; then he directed the group to gather dirt, twigs and grass from the formerly tapu area to take back to the village and cook up as a brew. This concoction was then fed to all the people to demonstrate that the tapu had indeed been cleared.

My great-grandfather calls this work 'mahi patu taipo'. A taipo is a spirit, and generally an unwelcome one, so the above phrase translates as 'the work of destroying spirits' or perhaps 'ghostbusting'. This was a man of faith – Christian faith as well as faith in the beliefs of his ancestors. He makes this clear in his writings. He believes.

I offer this background as an introduction to the stories that follow, not as an explanation for them. We make no attempt to explain the stories you will find within this book. They have been told to us and we merely wish to retell them as a record of the genuine experiences of a range of New Zealanders.

There are many things in this world that we find difficult to explain, although traditionally every community, culture and civilisation around the world has developed ways to explain and understand most things. All societies develop frameworks that allow for the unseen and the unheard. However, the age of science has challenged us to abandon our ancient understandings and instead place our faith in a more reasonable view of the world.

The metaphysical, the spiritual and the transcendental are not logical phenomena and all are too easily discarded by the modern scientific mind. Perhaps it is absurd that, at the dawn of the 21st century, we still cling to our somewhat primitive and undefined beliefs in the supernatural but, by the same token, we need to raise the debate on spirituality out of the incense-filled living rooms of shamans and fortune-tellers.

Each and every one of us has a personal account or a family story about

INTRODUCTION

ghosts, hauntings, ethereal misfortune, taipo or jimmies that we can recount as an entertaining 'strange but true' contribution to dinner conversation. Their retelling often belies the personal origin of those stories, but at the same time they are our own genuine stories.

When the events recalled in each of the following stories originally took place, the relevant protagonist was generally left in a confused state of mind. On the one hand he or she was firmly convinced that what just happened did in fact happen: that the image of the waka was clearly visible on the river, or that the rapid drop in temperature between rooms was distinct and uncanny.

But on the other, they were left with the head-shaking perplexity a whisker this side of scepticism that rallies together the rational thought processes, bringing them to bear upon the recent events and providing a list of sober alternatives. The waka may simply have been mist on the water, and a room that collects no sunlight will of course be a bit chilly.

This book attempts to capture the moment before the doubt sets in.

Tahu Potiki

The Hunter

This story took place just a few years ago. The man who passed it on to me doesn't believe in ghosts. Yet he can't explain what he saw.

I was about 14 or so when Dad and I headed into the bush to have a bit of a hunt. It was about Easter; the stags were grunting away in the bush in the hills behind the farm.

There was one stag with a huge 18-point rack that Dad had spotted a couple of times over the years way up in the back of the bush block. Real rough country. Dad reckoned the old fella was getting to the end of his days, and decided it was time he was taken as a trophy.

The two of us took the Land Rover to the end of the overgrown forestry track that ran back to where the ground suddenly tilted up to the clouds. We left the truck and started up the ridge on foot. Dad had his old .303 and a pack with food, sleeping bag and billy in it. I had my sleeping bag and the tent fly. The weather was cold but there hadn't been much rain, and we were planning on being out for only one night.

Dad was in a hurry to get to a camping spot, set it up and have a go at pinpointing the big stag for an early-morning stalk. I guess we climbed solidly for a couple of hours. I was getting pretty tired when we reached a flat area.

'This'll do us,' Dad said.

Boy, was I ready to rest up – but no such luck. Dad gave me the billy and sent me down a gully to get water while he put up the tent fly.

Dinner that night was baked beans and sausages cooked in a pan over the open fire and washed down with sweet tea. I don't think I've ever had a better meal.

It was getting cold. Dad had the fire stoked up and was sitting on a log sipping his tea and listening to the big stag telling the world who was boss. I'd been around deer since I was a kid. I could tell that this fella was a bit further away than he sounded, but he was a big one.

Anyway, I was getting cold, so I said goodnight to Dad and crawled into my sleeping bag under the tent fly. The fly was just a sheet of nylon, with a central cord attached to a couple of trees at either end. Side loops were pinned to the ground with broken twigs. The ends were open, so as I lay in my warm bag I could watch the flames of the fire.

I soon dozed off and I have no idea how long I was asleep, but when I opened my eyes, Dad wasn't alone. There was a man sitting next to him on the log. The fire was quite bright – there was plenty of dry wood and Dad was pretty liberal with it – so I could see well.

Dad had a mug of tea in one hand and the other man had a pipe in his mouth but no tea. The man was older than Dad, a Maori, with a big beard that came halfway down his chest. He had on a big thick jacket and a wide-brimmed hat.

I didn't really think there was anything strange about the guy's presence. I just assumed he was another hunter who had seen our fire and come over to pass the time. Funny thing, though, was that they weren't talking to each other. But I guess it is only odd in hindsight, because Dad wasn't a great talker at the best of times. He could sit for hours without saying a word.

Anyway, I was 14, growing like a bamboo shoot and tired, as all 14-year-olds seem to be. I just closed my eyes and went back to sleep.

In the morning the stranger was gone, and so was Dad. He had warned me that if he heard the stag roaring early he would just take off after it. I was to get up, put the billy on and take the camp down. If he got the animal he would come back and take me to have a look, otherwise he would just come back mid-morning.

I knew enough from previous expeditions to know that stalking a roaring stag is a solitary experience.

There was no sound of the big fella roaring, just a few smaller stags a long way away. I had the camp all broken down and packed up except for the tea things when Dad came back about 10 o'clock.

'Too smart for me,' he said as he put his rifle down and poured a mug of stewed tea.

'Where's the other chap?' I asked. I'd left my mug out so I could offer him a tea as well.

'What other chap?' Dad looked at me blankly.

'The old guy who was sitting next to you on the log last night.'

Dad looked at me as if I had lost my marbles.

'There was no one else here, Steve. Just you and me. You must have had a dream or something.'

But it had been so real. I argued with Dad, which was something I don't think I had ever really done before.

'Dad, I woke up. You were sitting there with a mug of tea and the old Maori guy was sitting beside you. He had pipe in his mouth, big brown beard down to his chest. Big hat – sorta cowboy one, but all rough. He had great big thick jacket on. There was plenty of light from the fire for me to see.'

Suddenly Dad was looking a bit strange. He tossed the remains of his tea away, stood up and had everything packed in about a minute. 'Come on, let's go.'

So off we went down the hill at a rate of knots. We got to the Land Rover in record time and what with having to open all the gates on the way out I never got a chance to ask Dad what was going on.

Later, after all the chores, I cornered him in the kitchen.

'Who was the man, Dad?' I asked him point blank.

He looked at me strangely and shrugged.

'His name was Toby Wensell. He used to be a bushman and possumer. Lived over the other side, but worked all through here.'

'Why did you say he wasn't there last night?' I was puzzled.

Dad sort of looked at the ceiling for a minute.

'Because he went missing in the bush before you were born. They think he had a heart attack or a fall or something. They never found his body.'

'Could still be alive,' I said.

'He'd be over a hundred years old,' said Dad.

'But I saw him!' I insisted.

'And I didn't!' said Dad firmly. 'I think we'll just leave it there, Steven. He only called me Steven when I was in his bad books. I shut up.

That Sunday we went to church for the first time in years.

The House that Jack Built

Barry from Greymouth was profoundly affected by the experience of a young couple, good friends of his, whose lives went suddenly downhill after they moved into their dream home.

We'll call them Jack and Maureen. They were a typical young Kiwi couple: married when he was 20, she 18 and six months' pregnant, barely showing in her wedding finery.

Both West Coasters, they wed in Hokitika and set up house a few kilometres out of town. Jack worked for a local contractor driving earth-moving equipment; Maureen gave up her job in a shop to look after their child. After two years living in a rented house they bought a 10-hectare block of land backing onto bush on which to build their dream home. Jack, his brother David and good friend Ray, who was a builder, worked on the house.

The house that Jack built wasn't a grand affair, but it had three bedrooms, a large lounge, a practical kitchen and a view down to the sea. It was built in wood, on a small terrace levelled by Jack driving one of his boss's dozers.

Jack and Maureen were soon in their new home: a happy young couple with a toddler, Mary, and another baby on the way. They were very well matched and we could all see a long and happy life ahead for them and the three children they planned to have.

But things went wrong almost from the moment they moved into their home.

At first they were little things. Mary became unsettled and began to cry constantly. Sleep was at a premium and no solution was forthcoming from the family doctor. There were sleeping tablets and Valium, but nothing helped. Tempers began to fray. Jack started to drink more. His long nights in the pub and his constant late arrivals home to his stressed wife and crying daughter caused frequent fights. Maureen often wore sunglasses on rainy days and high collars when the sun shone.

It soon became obvious to family, friends and neighbours that all was far from well.

I called in to see Jack and Maureen on my way south at the start of the whitebaiting season. Things obviously weren't good. The pair of them were at each other's throats the whole time. They both looked pale, haggard and skinny as hell. Maureen had big black circles under her eyes and I noticed bruises on her arms and neck. Jack was normally so easy going but he was wound as tight as a spring.

Anyway, Jack and I headed down to the pub and I noticed a lot of the locals kept their distance. That wasn't the way things had been a few months before. Last time I'd been here he'd been the life and soul of the party. Not now.

I found out later that Jack had been involved in a lot of arguments, even started a couple of fights. He had been banned from the pub for a month at one stage.

The night wasn't what you would call a pleasant one. I got very little sleep. They were fighting, Mary was crying and on top of that, things just didn't feel right in that house. I didn't realise it then but, looking back, it wasn't just the fighting, it was something else as well. A bad atmosphere.

I wasn't very keen to call in on my way back from the Arawhata three months later but I did. After all, Jack was one of my oldest mates. I had all sorts of ideas at the back of my mind that I'd been mulling over in the weeks I'd been down on the river. I'd figured that counselling might help them. I'd had a sticky patch with my wife Sharon a couple of years before. We sought help and got things sorted out pretty well.

So I called in, and I couldn't believe it. What a mess. The house was plain filthy. Dirty dishes were stacked in the sink and all over the bench, mud and rubbish covered the floor. There were dirty clothes overflowing out of the laundry, the kids looked and smelled as if they hadn't seen a bath in weeks. Jack was wild-eyed, Maureen was crying, Mary was crying, baby Andrew was crying.

I didn't stay, although they invited me to. I just told them I had to get back to Sharon and the kids as I'd been away so long. I didn't mention the counselling – I felt that if I opened my mouth Jack would deck me, best mate or no.

I was back home maybe two weeks when Ray rang from Hoki to say that Maureen had taken the kids and gone to her parents'. Jack was alone in the house. He'd chucked his job and was acting like a crazy man.

Ray told me he'd gone up to see him one night after Maureen had left. Jack had greeted him at the door with a rifle in his hand. He was almost raving, saying things like 'I'm not going to let them get me!' Real paranoid stuff.

Ray got scared. He went to see Jack's old man, Ted. Ted told Ray that

Jack had warned him to stay away from the place. Ted had talked to the local cop but he had said he couldn't do anything because Jack hadn't actually threatened anyone.

I talked it over with Sharon and we decided I had to try to get Jack out of the house, bring him back to our place, maybe get him a session with the guy we had seen. See if we could help sort things out. He was a mate – I couldn't just leave him there alone, although the thought of the rifle scared the hell out of me. He wasn't the Jack I thought I knew so well.

My brother Paul also knew Jack and he said he would come down with me. We agreed that if we had to, we'd knock him out and drag him back with us.

We got to Jack's place about nine on a Friday night. It was dark and there wasn't a light on, although his ute was out front. Paul and I were as jumpy as possums on a hot plate. It wouldn't have taken much to make us turn around and head straight home. I don't mind admitting I was bloody scared.

But we got out of the car, said 'Let's do it!' and went to the door. I called out: 'Jack! It's me, Bazza. Are you in there, mate?' There wasn't a squeak from inside.

The door was not locked so I opened it and we went in. I tried the lights in the lounge but no joy. We found out later that the power had been cut off a couple of weeks before.

The smell was the first thing that hit both of us. The place stank.

All the curtains were pulled closed and the house was as black as pitch. Neither of us could see a thing. I fished out my lighter and flicked it on, and about the same time I heard this little voice. It was like a kid talking.

'Is that really you, Baz?' the voice said. I could barely recognise it as Jack's.

'Of course it's me, mate!' I replied. I was so relieved to have found him alive. 'Where are you?' I still couldn't see a thing.

'I'm here,' came the little voice again, and then we saw him. He was huddled in a corner behind a chair with a rifle across his knees.

I've never seen anything like it. It was like looking at the pictures of kids in concentration camps or starving kids in Africa. Jack was all eyes. I mean it. They were huge – they seemed to take up half his head. The rest of him was hair – long greasy hair and a wild beard. He looked like Charles Manson.

'I can't let them get me, Baz!' he babbled. He was crying. I don't know what I said exactly – something like, 'They can't get you now we're here, mate!'

Jack was exactly like a frightened child. He let Paul take the rifle; the old .303 was loaded and cocked.

I got Jack to his feet. He was as light as a feather, all skin and bone, and he stank. Later, when we got him home to our place, Sharon burned his clothes, that's how bad they were.

Paul and I didn't muck around. We just bundled Jack into the car and got out of there. He was lying on the back seat crying his heart out. I tell you, if we'd run into a cop on the way north, I'd have lost my licence for a couple of years. The old Valiant was valve-bouncing all the way.

Sharon called our doctor while Paul and I stripped Jack, put him in the bath and scrubbed the hell out of him. We had him out, dried off and into bed when Doc arrived.

'Severe mental stress, sleep deprivation, nervous breakdown perhaps.' Doc gave us some sedatives for Jack and told us that what he needed was sleep. He would come back the next day.

We gave Jack a couple of pills and he just curled up like a baby. He was still crying when he went under. I drew first watch and sat with him for a couple of hours, then Paul took over until dawn. He didn't wake up until two in the afternoon. Doc had called about 10 in the morning and told us to let him sleep.

When Jack woke he looked calmer. The tears had stopped and his voice was normal. He seemed tired, and kind of lost, but at least he sounded like Jack again.

Doc came by and saw him in the afternoon. 'He's going to be okay I think. Plenty of sleep, good food, vitamins.'

We felt such relief. Sharon cooked up a big meal and Jack hooked into it as if he hadn't eaten for weeks. And judging by the way he looked in the bath, he hadn't. He didn't talk much, just ate and crashed out again.

Next day he started talking – spilling his guts is more like it. He didn't have a name for what had happened. The things that were after him ('them!') had been around ever since he had moved into the new house. Maureen had felt it too.

'I don't think I ever had a full night's sleep in that place,' Jack told me. 'Never. I'd just drift off and then I'd wake up sweating, scared to death, staring at the shadows. We started to sleep with the lights on and I had the deer rifle under the bed. All the doors were locked, the windows closed. But I didn't even know what I was scared of.'

He told us that after Maureen had left he was terrified of staying in the house, but too scared to leave.

We must have talked for hours over the next few days. I had some leave due from work so I took it. I drove Jack down to Maureen's parents' place the next weekend. Maureen and the kids looked great. There were lots of cuddles and kisses. The old Jack was definitely coming back. Maureen wanted him to stay, so I left him and shot home again.

At work on the Monday I was telling a couple of the blokes what had happened. Tony, one of my workmates, just sat there nodding as he listened. Tony's half Maori, born and bred on the Coast. I've known him all my life – we went to school, hunted and whitebaited together, played rugby in the same team, went to each other's 21sts, weddings. We were and are good mates.

Anyway, Tony just about floored me when he suddenly said, 'I know what the problem is.'

I picked my chin up off the floor.

'What?'

'Spirits, mate. The old people. I'll bet you a case of grog it's the spirits – a tapu on the place.'

'You mean the house is haunted?' I said.

'Basically, yeah. We can fix that easy.'

I sat there with the rest of the guys like a stuffed dummy but Tony was treating it as if it were an everyday kind of thing.

'Yeah, I'll speak to Dad. He and the old fellas will put it right. No problem.'

A few days later a convoy headed south. We had half a dozen cars all packed with elders from Tony's tribe. In Hoki there were another couple of cars. We picked up Jack and Maureen, and Sharon, Paul, Tony and his wife Tina and I all crammed into my old Valiant. We got to Jack's place about noon.

The rest of us stood and watched as Tony's dad, Danny, and the old people took over. They went into the house and spoke words and chanted and sang. Then they walked back up into the bush and did more of the same. I guess it took maybe a couple of hours, then they all came back to the cars.

Danny came over to where we were standing.

'It's all fixed,' he said, and explained what had caused the problem. Apparently on the hill behind the house there were some old Maori graves. Like a lot of gravesites, the area was sacred and a tapu was put on it. A creek flowed down the hill and went under where the house was. Spirits have an affinity with water and they can travel down streams. Danny said that was why the house was 'haunted' – it was the influence of the tapu. Anyway, the tohunga or Maori priest and the elders had lifted the tapu.

'Should have come and seen us when it started, Jack,' Danny said.

Jack just shook his head. 'I didn't know what was happening.'

'Won't happen again. It's all laid to rest.' Tony was very reassuring.

Thank God for that, I thought.

A week later we had working bee at Jack and Maureen's. Cleaned the place up, painted and papered. Tony organised a big hangi, we got in a few kegs and had a house-warming party.

Jack and Maureen and the kids moved back in. No problem. They've got four kids now and have even added a couple more rooms. He's got his own business, and life is pretty damned good.

Letting Go

This tale is from the East Coast of the North Island. The man who told it to me has been a widower for 10 years. In that time, although he has been in other relationships, he has never had another woman stay in his house, apart from his two grown-up daughters. He regards the house as being a special place where he and the love of his life made their home. Arthur is a Christian in the true sense of the word, although he does not belong to a particular church. This has been his only supernatural experience.

My marriage to Vanita had been a very fulfilling one and we had two beautiful daughters together. We had been married for 16 years when Vanita succumbed to cancer.

After Vanita died I went through a long period of mourning – very long in fact, and on several occasions I came close to committing suicide. I wanted to join her, but at the same time I knew she would not have wanted me to take this way out.

Gradually I came back to the land of the living. It was perhaps two and a half years after her death when I learned to smile again and all my friends breathed big sighs of relief.

Some told me later that they had even had secret meetings among themselves to discuss how to help me. Looking back, I can see how there was a pattern to their unannounced visits. Whoever was 'on watch' as it were would drop in at odd times, but more particularly in the evenings after work.

I am not a big drinker and I noticed that these friends would often 'drop in' at times when I knew they were normally at the club or the pub. I'm very grateful to them. If they read this they will know who they are. I think their visits and unspoken support saved me.

I slowly settled into my bachelor existence and found that the pain gradually numbed a little bit. I was comfortable with my memories in 'our place'. It wasn't a maudlin thing – this was no shrine, it was just a comfortable home full of memories.

I began a friendship with a lady who was a widow and who lived in a small town not far away. I visited her often but she understood why I never invited her to my house. She had been a widow for 10 or 12 years but she had moved house.

'Three years,' she said to me. 'You should live there for three years before you leave. That gives you and your wife's spirit time to heal.'

At the end of three years I didn't want to move. I was selfishly comfortable. My married daughter Alice and her husband and children came to stay often. Eva, my unmarried daughter, came every other fortnight and she used to bring her friends with her. The house was big enough for everyone. If I had moved, it would have been to a smaller place, and then everyone would not have been able to stay.

It was Eva who experienced something first, and it happened just before she got married. That was three years after Vanita's death. Eva came to visit for a weekend to talk over her wedding plans with me. She was going to get married in Gisborne, her fiancé's home town. I was quite happy with that.

Anyway, on the Friday night we sat up late and talked. When it was time for bed she went off to her old bedroom, which I had made up for her. At some stage I heard her get up in the night and I assumed she had gone to the bathroom.

In the morning when we met in the kitchen Eva looked tired.

'Couldn't you sleep?' I asked, thinking that maybe the excitement of her wedding was playing on her mind.

'No, Pop,' she said. 'I was so cold. I had to get up and get more blankets for the bed. Even then I was cold.'

I wondered how that could be. The house was such a warm house. This was early summer and the nights were not even cool, let alone cold. I had made up the bed with two blankets and a counterpane, and there was a quilt on the end of the bed as well.

We had breakfast and Eva spent the day catching up with friends. We had a gathering at her aunt's that night for a hangi and a pre-wedding party. It was a late night and Eva and I came home in the small hours of the morning.

I was awoken when it was still dark. Eva was standing by the bed.

'Pop, I can't sleep in that bed. It's just too cold. Can I get in with you?'

I said of course and she did. We sat up and talked until dawn. Later that day Eva left for Gisborne and it was that night that I had my experience.

I had spent the day working in my garden and smoking eels in my big smokehouse. The wedding breakfast was to be a combination of traditional Maori kai and European fare. Several of the whanau were busy with preparations. We had some wild pigs penned up on my brother's farm. It was going to be a big affair.

That night I was very tired and went to bed early. I worked at a fruit processing plant and we started at six, which meant I had to be up at five.

I had been sound asleep but woke in the night freezing cold. The bed was like ice. I shivered and sat up, and as I did so I just about shouted.

There, standing right beside the bed, was a figure. It was white – sort of blue-white. It had no features but was the shape of a person. There was no indication whether it was male or female.

'Who are you? What do you want?' I asked. I was beyond fright for some reason. There seemed to be a calming influence coming from somewhere.

There was no spoken reply, but I know these words came to me. They went like this: 'I am cold. I want to lie in your bed with you.' I heard those words in my head and the voice was Vanita's. 'Can I lie in your bed?' her voice was asking.

'Yes,' I said. I was totally and absolutely unafraid for some reason. 'Yes, you can lie in my bed.' I pulled back the covers and moved over. When Vanita had been alive she always slept on the left of the bed. After she died I had moved across there for some reason.

I swear that I felt the mattress move as if a weight had come down on the bed. I couldn't see the white figure but there was a presence there.

I didn't want to look so I just lay with my eyes closed, and gradually the cold started to go away. I fought sleep but eventually I must have dropped off.

When I woke at five in the morning I was over on the right side of the bed. There was nothing in or on the left side to indicate that anyone other than I had ever been in the bed. The morning was warm, even at that early hour. I got up, showered, dressed and went to work.

At some stage during the day I was talking to one of my old friends. Kore had been a friend of my father's. He was a tohunga, and I respected his words of wisdom, so I told him what had happened to Eva and myself.

'I think Vanita's spirit wanted to see her daughter before she married. And she wanted to see you and share your bed one last time before she moved on. Sometimes spirits don't leave straight after death. They stay to look after the ones they leave behind, and when the time is right they move on. Sometimes they don't even know they are dead. I can ask her spirit to leave and move on if you want, but I think she has done that already.'

'She can stay if she wants,' I replied.

Kore just smiled and nodded. 'That is a sign that you are healed, Arthur. I think she knows that and has gone on.'

LETTING GO

In bed that night I lay waiting, trying in vain to stay awake. But I never saw the white shape again. I never felt that intense cold.

That was seven years ago and I think my old friend was right. Vanita's spirit has moved on. Perhaps she stayed those first years to help me fight my fight and keep me from harm. I would like to think so.

Where No Birds Sing

There are places on this earth that do not welcome people. Death Valley, the Arctic and Antarctic, the great deserts of Africa and Australia are such places. In these cases it is the climate and the terrain that make the areas inhospitable.

There are other unwelcoming places, however, where climate is not a factor. Places where something else is at work – something that causes the hair on the back of your neck to tingle and your pulse rate to climb. Something that makes you hurry away, icy sweat trickling down your spine, even in the heat of the day.

I have found two such places in my life. One was an ancient battlefield in Scotland, my ancestral home. It was a mountain valley in the Highlands where thousands of men had died in a bloody and ultimately futile battle. Here it seemed that the very earth and stones had absorbed the agony of the mass suffering along with the blood of the warriors. Over the hundreds of years that followed, this place seemed to release the horror afresh into the atmosphere as an almost tangible thing. I was only too eager to leave after only a few minutes.

The other place was a small valley in Fiordland. As a hunter I used to be a frequent visitor to the region. I have been back many times since my experience but I will never again visit this particular valley.

It was a long hunt. My companions and I had two weeks on the hunting block. We had great weather for the time of year and there were plenty of animals to be found, including some excellent red deer-wapiti cross bulls with fine racks.

By day three our legs were starting to get used to the hills again. Eyes were sharp and lungs had acclimatised to their diet of fresh, fresh air.

Hunting alone, I had spent a long morning gaining height, making my way up a steep ridge. I gained the rocky outcrop I was climbing for at about 11 o'clock. For a while I sat motionless, glassing the valley ahead of and below me.

The valley was short and densely forested. It had a steep floor that ended in a tussock basin above which I was sitting. I gazed around the clearings and into the bush edges. There was nothing moving. I then sat and scanned the areas of the basin that I could see from my vantage point. Again, nothing.

I decided to climb higher to give myself a better view into the basin. From where I was sitting it looked like prime territory for a big stag to be holding his harem of hinds.

I dropped below the skyline and started climbing, stopping every 20 paces or so to peer over the lip and look and listen for a stag roaring. There was no sound but the wind.

High enough at last, I lay on my belly and spent half an hour glassing every inch of the basin. Nothing. I was disappointed. This really was a perfect spot for a herd of animals to be on such a day. There was water, a small meadow and a clump of trees for shelter.

I decided to go down and see if there was any animal sign on the floor of the basin. There was always the chance that I could come across something if I made my way down the valley. If the deer had come under pressure from hunters in the days before we arrived on the block, perhaps they were holing up in bush during the daylight hours. Technically, we were the first here for the trophy season, but poaching was and is rife come autumn in the south.

The basin had virtually no sign and what was there was old. The few deer tracks here ran into the basin from one side and out the other. There was no sign of animals coming up or down the valley.

This was odd. To my mind, the only reasons deer would avoid moving up and down the valley would be if the unseen terrain under the trees was impassable. Deer are like humans in that respect – they choose the easiest possible route from A to B. That is often their downfall.

I had a late lunch and a boil-up at the spring-fed tarn in the basin before I started down the valley.

The going was surprisingly easy at first. There were no deer trails but the ground under the canopy was quite open. I moved slowly, rifle across my chest, eyes peeled for a movement in the shadows. There was none.

I went on, dropping quite quickly. The undergrowth was now reasonably heavy but still no great problem. I couldn't understand why there wasn't a deer trail. I alternated between walking down the steep creekbed and scrambling through the bracken fern and bush lawyer when the creek turned into one of its frequent waterfalls or tumbling rapids.

About mid-afternoon I concluded that there really were no deer here. I stopped for a brew in a small clearing. There was a big bluff above me and huge rocks had come crashing down at some stage. They littered the clearing. Broken trees showed where they had crashed down the slope before coming to rest. I sat on one while I waited for the water to boil.

WHERE NO BIRDS SING

There was no wind down here and, I now noticed for the first time, no birdsong either. That was weird. Normally when you move through the bush, robins and fantails, in particular, accompany you. Your movements through the bush send insects into the air, which attract these aerial acrobats to feed. Many people new to the bush think that the birds just come to say gidday. I guess they do, but they have their own ulterior motives.

No birds. No deer. I had the feeling that this day was going to be an empty one. I didn't really mind. I had picked up a spiker for meat the day before and I had taken plenty of trophies in the past. I was just really pleased to be back in Fiordland. I had my brew and started down again.

I guess it was 10 minutes from my last stop that I started to feel it. At first it was the silence. It was deeper than it had been before. It's hard to explain but the bush isn't really a silent place. The wind moves the trees, branches clack together, leaves rustle, birds sing, streams gurgle and hiss. It's quite noisy really.

But somehow here what little sound there was seemed sort of muffled. I started feeling that something wasn't right. There was nothing really obvious – it was just a nagging feeling in the back of my mind.

It's not as if I'm not used to the bush and being alone in it. I have always preferred hunting alone and I'm pretty successful. I have the ability to read the bush, interpret the noises, pick the spots where a deer might be standing straining its senses to identify the intruder. My eyes are good at reading movement, seeing the twitch of an ear or the quiver in a shadow as an animal transfers its weight ready for flight.

So I guess you could say I'm an experienced hunter and bushman. I knew exactly where I was on the map, knew where camp was, and I had plenty of daylight left. I tried to analyse what the problem was and with a shock it came to me that there was a definite feeling of dread or expectation in the air. I don't know how else to describe it, although I've tried so many times since. Something was going to happen, that was the feeling.

I've never hunted a predatory beast but in retrospect I imagine that the sensation I was experiencing was like that of a hunter following a wounded lion into a patch of thorn. My heart was pounding, my mouth was dry and my eyes ached from straining to see something I knew wasn't ever going to be seen. If it had been anywhere else in the world I would have broken into a jog but in this country that would more than likely get you a broken leg or worse.

I now desperately wanted to get down to where this valley joined the main one but I forced myself to move on at a steady pace and not rush. I must admit I kept the rifle in my hands, the bolt at half close on a round.

The air around me was really charged. It was as if there were an electrical current flowing through it. It was like the moments before a thunderstorm when the air is heavy and thick, but the sky I could see through the trees was bright, clear blue and almost cloudless. The hair on my neck and my arms was tingling by this time. Imagination! I told myself. Don't let it get to you. I kept on moving, scolding myself every time I started to let the sensations get through to me.

The working over I gave myself did help. Now the valley was wider and the fern a lush green carpet. Unfortunately four feet under the carpet was a minefield of dead falls so the going was slow. The creek wasn't an option because the banks were steep and it had got quite deep. My feet were still dry and I intended to keep them that way.

I battled my way through a mass of fern and old tree trunks, trying not to panic. The air was so thick I was at times struggling to keep my breathing even. My heart was pounding in my chest and in my ears. So this is what the start of a heart attack feels like, I remember thinking to myself at one stage. But I ploughed on, slipping and sliding on rotten moss and lichen-covered logs.

Every time I crashed down I would drag myself back to my feet and start off again. I would have to say that I was as close to panic as I have ever been in my life. It was a struggle to keep a lid on things. All the time the atmosphere was pressing down on me like a huge soft enveloping weight.

Anxiety attack was a doctor friend's diagnosis years later when I told him about my experience. I had to agree. I sure as hell was having an anxiety attack, but what was bringing it on was not all in my head. I know that for an absolute fact. I was wondering if I would ever get clear of this place. The valley now seemed to be without end, although my watch told me I had only been in it two hours. It felt like I'd been there half my life.

Then I sensed a change in the atmosphere. Gradually as I moved on down the valley I felt as if the air was growing thinner, the weight or pressure that had been closing in on me was lessening. The sound was changing too. The creek was louder and so were the wind and the trees.

I moved on and with every step I took, the sense of dread that had been gnawing at me gradually fell away. The dead falls and fern gave way to open bush and I soon came across a deer trail running diagonally across in front of me. I was back on the floor of the main valley. The creek I had been following flowed into the main stream just a few yards away from where I stood.

I think I gave a very audible 'Whew!' I found a clearing bordered by the main stream, with a log on the bank. I dropped my rifle and day bag, took my mug, filled it and set a fire lighter under it to brew a celebratory coffee. Whatever I had passed through, I had made it in one piece.

I was sitting there with my coffee when a huge stag suddenly appeared 20 feet upstream from me on the edge of the clearing. He stood looking at me while I put down my coffee and reached for the rifle, moving slowly, very slowly. I was half in shadow and he wasn't sure what I was. He obviously couldn't smell me or the coffee because the wind was blowing down the valley from behind him.

I reached the rifle and started to bring it up to my shoulder, again moving so slowly. Hip shooting at 20 feet while you're sitting down only works in movies. But despite my stealth the stag sensed the movement and broke, leaping away towards the place I had just come from. I had a flash of rump in my scope, then he was gone into the undergrowth. I went to put the rifle down – I wasn't going to chase him. He was gone.

Suddenly the stag was coming back. He was going at full tilt, cutting across in front of me on an angle to head back upstream, reversing his original course. As he hit the edge of the clearing only a few yards away I had the shot and brought him down cleanly.

That stag was the biggest of the trip: a wide, heavy 18-pointer. But my mind keeps coming back to it: why did he not keep going? He was away scot-free, but he turned and came back. Did he sense what I had experienced? Was that why no deer went through what seemed at first glance a perfect little valley? For whatever reason, that animal had turned away from the little valley and had died.

Because I had a fine trophy I spent a couple of days around camp cooking and doing odd jobs. I didn't tell the other guys about my valley. They would have accused me of a hefty dose of imagination. I even began to wonder myself if it had actually happened, even though I knew it had. The mind is great at blocking out some things.

It was on the evening of the second day that I had an ally, however unwilling, after John came into camp just on dark. He was as white as a ghost. It wasn't raining but he was soaking wet. He dropped his gear and poured himself a stiff drink, then he started to tell us about 'this place' where there were no birds and where he had felt terrified. The others started to give John heaps – until I told them I had been there too.

'We'll take you there tomorrow and you can see for yourselves,' I said and that shut them up for the night.

Next day John and I took the other two to the place where I had shot the stag.

'Up there,' I said, pointing out the direction they should take. John and I stood there and watched them march off like soldiers into battle. No way were Frank and Evan going to be sucked in by this rubbish.

John and I sat on my log and had just brewed up when the other two were back. They had only gone a couple of hundred yards before they had decided that things definitely weren't right with that part of the world.

We didn't talk much about it after that.

I've never forgotten that particular spot in the bush – the spot where no birds sing – and despite having been down to Fiordland several times since, I have never been tempted to go up that particular valley. I don't think I ever will.

The Walkers

This tale was told to me by a man who has lived in the same house on the same West Coast South Island beach for all of his 80 years. His mother and father had lived there for 40 years before that.

The view from Doug's house is of an expanse of beach that runs unbroken, but for river mouths and small estuaries, for some 20 kilometres in either direction. It is a view that Doug never tires of, and one that is as familiar to him as the face that stares back at him every morning in the mirror.

It was about 50 years ago it happened. We had a terrible storm out in the Tasman – the weather was the worst in living memory.

In those days I was working for a timber milling company. For a week there had been no work in the bush. It wasn't just the rain – that was something we could handle. It was the wind. Trees and branches were coming down all over the place. Roofs had been ripped off, power and telephone poles were down. It was a real mess.

Mavis and I tied down everything on our property that could have blown away. We were lucky that we didn't get the wind quite as badly as some houses closer to town. When Dad built the house he used a horse and team to drag some big driftwood logs into a line between the house and the sand. Whenever the westerly blew, the sand driven up the beach was caught by the logs, and over the years the dunes had built up. They weren't high, but they formed a lip that bounced the wind over us.

On the Saturday a railways gang arrived to keep the line cleared. One of them told us that a coastal ship had capsized as it tried to get across the bar down at Greymouth. It was a local vessel that ran between Grey and Westport and around to Nelson, Picton and Wellington. He didn't know how many crew there had been, just that they had all been drowned.

There were a lot of tragedies on the coast in those days. There were always accidents in the mines and in sawmilling. Since the storm had started about a week before, one of the local miners had been killed when his car was caught in a slip. Two young men from up the way had foolishly gone to lift a flounder net in a river lagoon and got tipped out of their dinghy by the wind. They drowned and their bodies had not been found.

So it was a pretty glum gathering that Saturday night. Even the local policeman came in for the after-hours session, which he never had before. I think the storm had just worn everyone out. I didn't stay long as Mavis was cooking a big meal and we were having neighbours over. The storm had taken the roof off their kitchen and they were sort of camping in the rest of the house, cooking on the open fire in the living room. We decided they needed a good old-fashioned coast meal.

Bob and I picked up his wife, June, on our way home. We were walking of course – not many of us had cars then. Anyway, the three of us were dressed in our oilskins, all bent into the wind and sea spray. June was only a little thing so Bob and I each had one of her arms to stop her being blown over.

When we got close to our house the wind was not as bad. We could all stand up straight. 'Lucky you,' said Bob, shaking his head. 'I thought yours would have been the first place to blow away!' Our dunes didn't stop the spray though – everything was soaked. The air for a half mile back from the beach was as wet as a West Coast drizzle.

We had our dinner and a few hands of gin rummy and a beer and talked for a while about the storm, the shipwreck down at Grey and other things, then Bob and June went off home. Mavis and I did the dishes and were about to get ready for bed when we realised the wind had stopped. For the first time in a week, a week and a half, it had stopped, and apart from the roaring of the sea there was almost silence.

I went out on the porch and rolled a smoke. There was still spray in the air, but it was normal, not wind driven. I could see the clouds, way up high racing across the sky from Australia, heading towards South America. There was moonlight. It had been there before no doubt, but the sea spray had meant we couldn't see it.

Mavis came out and stood beside me. 'Want to take a walk and stretch the legs?' I asked her. She shook her head – she wasn't keen but she told me to go. I pulled on my coat and gumboots and let our old collie, Ben, out of the laundry, which had been his kennel since the big wind had begun.

Out onto the beach we went. It was about 10 o'clock at night I guess. The big waves were pounding in but there was no wind. Old Ben was like a puppy, running around all over the place.

I suppose we walked for two miles, which was a short walk for us. I just didn't trust the weather and didn't want to be too far from home if the storm came crashing back.

I was just about to turn back towards home when I saw some other people walking on the beach, coming towards me from the south. The moon was quite bright and I could see them reasonably clearly. There were seven of them walking in a line abreast across the sand and shingle. There was a lot of driftwood lying on the beach, but they were just walking over it.

I was surprised to see other people out on the beach at that hour. I mean, there were no houses that far down. Even on fine mornings and evenings when I'd take Ben for a walk there would be no one out on the beach most times.

I guess the seven were a hundred yards away when old Ben started to make a noise. It was a funny sound I'd never heard him make before. He was standing staring down the beach at the approaching figures and he was half snarling. He turned and looked at me, then back at them. Then he gave me a yip and turned and bolted back up the beach. He stopped a few yards further up and barked at me again.

I asked him what was wrong but he just made that strange noise again. Ben had never been an aggressive dog – quite the opposite in fact. But here he was baring his teeth and the hair around his neck was sort of like a lion's mane, all sticking out. I turned to look back at the figures coming towards us. They were closer, still walking stretched across the beach, still just sort of walking over the driftwood, not around it.

Ben gave another yip and then he was off. I turned to watch him. He stopped a hundred yards further up and gave me a bark as if to say 'Come on!' Then he was off for home like a bullet.

I was reaching for my tobacco to roll a smoke. I figured I'd wait for these blokes – I could see they were blokes, they were close enough and the moon was bright enough for me to see their shapes quite plainly. They were all wearing oilskins and most had on sea-boots. One wore what looked like a life-jacket. They all had on caps or hats.

I was halfway through rolling the smoke when I suddenly felt a shiver run down my spine. I really shuddered and spilled my tobacco. I knew right then and there that I didn't want to be where I was – wasn't supposed to be where I was.

I turned and started to walk quickly back up the beach. I looked back after a few paces and they were still coming on as they had been before, just stretched across the beach. I kept walking, dodging the huge piles of driftwood and kelp that had been thrown up by the storm. I looked back again a few yards further on. They were still coming, and then I saw something that made me want to run. Only a minute before, I had been forced to go around a huge tree trunk with roots still attached. One of the figures had just walked right through it.

THE WALKERS

That did it for me. I cut off the beach to one of the many tracks that ran from sand to the road through the dunes. I don't really know if I was scared, or just completely and utterly bewildered – in some kind of shock. I got to the top of a sand dune and turned to look back.

They were walking on as they had been. They had taken no notice whatsoever of me. I just stood there. The nearest figure was 50 or 60 yards away; the rest spread out from him down almost to where the waves foamed in. They were level with me, then they were past and going away on up the beach. They seemed as solid as any people I had ever seen in my life, but as I watched they just walked through the logs and piles of kelp and rubbish as if it wasn't there. None of them deviated one step.

I didn't know what to do. Were they a threat, whoever – whatever – they were? Should I run home along the road in case they left the beach and went to my house?

I think the modern term for what I was experiencing is denial. I realised of course that if they were what my subconscious was telling me they were (which was impossible of course) then there was nothing I could do. Also, my mind was arguing, even if they were what I knew they couldn't possibly be, there was probably nothing to fear. Yes, that's how confused I was.

I managed to fumble together the worst smoke I've probably ever rolled in my life and eventually I got it going. I never took my eyes off them the whole time. They had been moving so quickly and relentlessly, I honestly don't think I could have stayed ahead of them on the sand, or outrun them on the road.

They were a long way up the beach when I suddenly decided I would go back down onto the sand and follow them. It wasn't a decision made through bravery. Curiosity had by now overcome fear and even confusion. There was something I could do to prove or disprove what my subconscious was trying to tell me.

I checked to see there was no one else walking up the beach, then I went down to the sand and started after the seven figures. They were away in the distance and I looked down at the sand where they'd been. The only footprints in the patches of sand between the shingle banks and storm debris were Ben's and mine. None of those seven sets of sea-boots had left a mark.

When I got back to the house they were almost gone. The moon was fading because the wind was coming back and the spray was starting to cloud everything again. Ben was under the verandah. He was overjoyed to see me. I let him spend the rest of the night in the house.

In bed later I told Mavis what I had seen. Now Mavis's mother was

37

some sort of clairvoyant or something similar. I remember thinking it was all pretty strange when I first met Mavis and her family. Her mother did tea-leaf readings and tarot and things. She offered to do my hands once but I wouldn't have a bar of it.

Mavis fortunately didn't follow in her mother's footsteps in that regard, which I am thankful for. However, she was a lot more tolerant of and had a lot better understanding of those sorts of things than I ever had or wanted to have. She thought about what I had told her for a little while. Then she said, 'They're just going home.'

'What do you mean?' I asked.

'Those poor boys who drowned on the bar. You saw their spirits going home to say goodbye to their families. Bob said they came from Westport. That's where they're going.'

We were halfway between Greymouth and Westport. If any live person wanted to take the easiest, most direct way, they would have to go past us. As for the spirits of the dead, I wasn't so sure. All I can remember 40 years later is the way that nothing stopped them, and the way that one bloke walked right through that great big tree stump as if it wasn't there.

I told Mavis not to mention this incident to anyone. I had a reputation for being a bit pragmatic and straightforward I suppose. I didn't want anyone thinking I was given to flights of fancy. Mavis may have mentioned it to her mother – I suspect she did – but no one else knew.

A couple of days later there was a piece in the newspaper on the wrecking of the *Kestrel*. There had been seven crew members on board, all drowned, and yes, they all came from up Westport way.

They say animals can sense things on another level to us. Had old Ben known that these seven figures on the beach were not alive? I guess we'll never know.

I had a funny feeling that after Mavis died she might appear for me. She didn't, perhaps because she died peacefully in bed in our home, with me there holding her hand. She didn't have to make her way home to the ones she loved, because she was already there.

The Right Way and the Wrong Way

John is a modern Maori. He is a sophisticated professional, university educated, well-travelled and not necessarily a great believer in the old ways, or in the superstitions of his people. However, in recent times his attitude has changed a little, and this particular incident has had more than a little to do with it.

I'd been away from my rehe or district for a couple of years, finishing my studies and working. As for many folk, Maori and Pakeha, there is often no work available at home, especially for those of us who are working in professional or white collar areas. It's not snobbery, it is simply a fact of life. It's unfortunate in that many of us lose touch with some essential part of ourselves when we move away. In particular, we lose a sort of earthy understanding of nature and maybe the history of things and the old ways seem to be lost to us - and that is a great shame. Anyway, I'd come to visit my whanau and have a bit of a holiday and catch up with friends – some of them I hadn't seen since the barefoot days of school, when every day was summer. Others I wanted to catch up with were older friends, people I'd grown up with as a youngster, who had a profound influence on who I had become. One of the latter group was Luke. He had seemed a wise old man when I was young. When I caught up with him again, I was suprised to find that he wasn't yet sixty.

On my visit with the old gang we did it all. We stayed in the pub playing pool and drinking until closing time. We partied up large, with a great big party and a hangi for all the whanau and friends. It felt very comfortable being back home. I knew inside, that yes, I had changed. I also knew that I wasn't ashamed of the changes. I promised myself that I would come back more often though, and never let myself get as distant again from my family and old friends. These were my people and my roots, and big city boy or not, I was proud to come from here.

Because there was a long weekend at the start of my break, I spent a lot of time with my younger friends in those first few days. When most of them were back at work in the following week, I caught up with some the older people, including Luke. Luke suggested that we go down the coast and have a fish and catch up. I thought it was a great idea. Now, they'd been having a drought down home for the best part of a year and this was a real drought day. The sun was beating down unmercifully when we set off in Luke's ute. The drive only took half an hour, and when we got to the fork in the shingle road, it was right to the rocks, or left to the lagoon. Luke stopped. 'How about we go for a look at the lagoon before we go fishing?' he asked. 'Haven't been over there for ages. Never know what we'll find, and it'll bring back a few memories. Remember when we all used to go floundering out there?' Did I ever remember that. It was one of my fondest childhood memories. There would be ten or twelve adults and kids, the big drag net, the bonfires on the beach. We'd have mussels and pipi and kina, and fresh flounder cooked on a piece of tin over a fire. It was the best kai in the world.

So, when Luke made the suggestion, I agreed readily. It would be another experience to bring back the past, another memory to carry away with me. He turned left and we ran down a series of dry dirt tracks towards the lagoon. He parked where the track ended at what had once been a favourite swimming hole in one of the many creeks that drained into the lagoon. The pool was a ten foot deep hole in the dust and shingle. 'Gosh she's dry. I've never seen it so bad!' said Luke as we got out of the truck and started off on foot to where we could see a distant patch of water.

What would normally have been the bottom of the lagoon, which was tidal in its lower reaches, was just cracked mud and shingle. 'Look at those!' Luke was pointing out the dead eels that were everywhere. 'Eels always find water,' he said, puzzled. I'd always thought so too. As kids out eeling with torches and spears, we had often seen slime trails on the grass on dewy nights, when the eels went overland.

Eels have a pretty big significance to us Maori, not only as a food source, but also from a spiritual standpoint. Different iwi have different views on them, but they are important in many ways.

As a former professional fisherman, Luke was disturbed to see dozens of decaying eels just lying in the dirt. There were birds feeding on them, big black birds. I didn't really pay much attention to the birds then. I have wished many times since that I had.

We were maybe half way to the water and getting to the high tide line when Luke stopped dead in his tracks, his head turned to one side, his eyes focused on something I couldn't see. He looked stunned, his face set then becoming distorted as he became agitated. He started having a discussion in Maori with someone or something I couldn't see. The conversation seemed one-sided to me. I couldn't hear any reply, but what Luke was saying was enough to make the hairs on the back of my neck stand up very straight.

He was saying things like, 'I didn't know it was wrong. Must we go back? What can we do to make it right?'

I was totally scared. I mean, there we were standing in the middle of a dust bowl in the blazing sun, and Luke was talking to something or someone that didn't exist, as far as I was concerned.

I thought for a moment that Luke might have been having a joke with me, pulling the city boy's leg. I could see though that this was no joking matter. The veins and muscles in his neck were really standing out, there was sweat on his face, and not from the sun, and to top it all off, he looked really upset. His words were making less and less sense to me, and I'm a Maori speaker from childhood. Then as suddenly as he had stopped, Luke started walking forward again and stopped a few paces further on.

'What's happening?' I asked.

'We have entered this place the wrong way,' he said. 'My ancestors are standing here. They are unhappy with us. They're talking to me.'

Once again, and as before, he started talking to thin air. Again, the one-sided conversation was about permission and making things right. Then Luke's language again sort of went into tongues that I couldn't understand. I was stunned and very uneasy. All of this was way outside my experience. I'd never seen a ghost that I knew of. I'd never felt a presence or anything like that. I can tell you that I felt a presence this time. It wasn't just Luke, it was like electricity in the air in the minutes before a lightning storm.

Luke started to recite a karakia or Maori prayer and that for me was the final straw. This sort of thing doesn't happen on bright, sunny twentieth-century days. I grabbed at his arm to draw him away. I'm a big guy and Luke is quite slight, but I couldn't move him. 'Come on Luke,' I was saying, probably yelling. I remember these big black birds flapping into the air. Luke's karakia was loud too. I was still pulling at his arm but he didn't move until his prayer was finished, then we staggered a bit and sort of propped each other up.

'It's okay,' Luke said. 'All fixed.'

'Like hell it's all fixed,' I said. 'I'm out of here.' I started back the way we had come. After a minute, Luke came with me.

'What the hell was that all about?' I asked him as we sent the black birds and dust flying.

'All my ancestors. They were lined up there. I had to speak to them. We came into this place from the wrong side. I forgot that we must never come this way. It is an old thing from our past. I just forgot and they stopped me to remind me. It's okay now.'

'Not for me,' I replied. Maybe I had been away too long. Maybe I could have handled things better, but I was genuinely scared. This whole thing was beyond my experience.

Luke and I got in the truck and left. We never did go fishing. We ended up in the pub, both shaken.

As for those black birds that were feeding on the dead eels. I forgot to ask Luke what they were. I've never seen any like them before. I know all manner of New Zealand birds. These were not black shags or hawks. They were big black birds the size of geese, like eagles or condor. I had never seen them before and I have never seen them since. The only birds I ever remember in that place before were seagulls and the odd magpie.

I haven't been back down south for a while. When I next do, I'm going to ask Luke about the birds and I'm going to ask him a lot of other questions. I'm not really sure I want the answers, but I think I owe it to myself and my people to at least ask.

The Laying on of Hands

The narrator of this story is a young man of Maori/Samoan/Irish heritage. A top rugby player from a family that includes several former All Blacks, he is looking beyond his career in the game, and preparing himself to follow his spiritual calling.

I was 18 when this happened. I was a big lad, working on weights, playing rugby and league, eating big, drinking probably more than was good for me. I'd made certain decisions in my life relatively early I guess. When rugby was over for me, I was going to become a kind of missionary, one who perhaps had a skill at helping heal physically and mentally damaged people.

My sister Alison, who was 16, had a friend. We'll call her Suzy. Suzy was, like Alison and me, mostly Maori. Like me, she had a Pakeha stepfather, or should I say a series of them. How many ever were married to her mother we never knew. There were kids everywhere at their place and they were always in trouble through lack of discipline or parenting.

Suzy lived in a ramshackle house in a bad part of our little township. She spent a lot of time with Alison at our place, and stayed over often, becoming like part of our family. There were only three of us plus Mum and Dad in our big house so another person was never a problem. Alison had two beds in her room anyway.

Mum was very house-proud and our place was always spotless. As kids, our behaviour was pretty good. The atmosphere was happy and friendly – welcoming, you could say. Suzy was never turned away, and that had a lot to do with what was to take place.

Suzy unfortunately had one very bad habit. She was a shoplifter and a petty thief. It was a behavioural problem that probably stemmed from her upbringing, but no one ever really pursued the cause to any great degree. The local police and social services tried to help, but things never seemed to get better. The influence of Alison and our family was considered good for Suzy, and unofficially she was encouraged to spend time with us. She never stole anything from our house and was always polite to everyone.

Perhaps at the end it was our influence, particularly that of Alison, that finally helped Suzy to vow seriously to break her 'habit'. I can remember the night she announced to us all that she was 'finished with all that stuff'.

We were all in the kitchen having dinner. Suzy, who had beautiful blonde hair to go with her permanent tan and brown eyes, sat there at the table and solemnly made her announcement. I think we just about all clapped her. There were lots of hugs and she really beamed; it was as if a weight had been lifted off her. She was radiant and very determined.

A week later, she was dead. After college one evening she was walking home with a bunch of other girls. Suzy waved goodbye, turned to cross the road, and a car hit her. No one ever knew if the car swerved into her, or if she stepped out in front of it. All anyone knew was that she was dead.

For our family it was as if we had lost a daughter and sister. We basically went into mourning along with Suzy's real family – or, not being totally unkind, several of them at least. Mum and Dad actually helped pay for some of the funeral.

It was maybe three weeks after Suzy was buried that strange things started to happen around our place. At first we all had our individual odd experiences but didn't think to compare notes. Only in retrospect did we realise just how many 'experiences' in total we had.

It started with just little things. For instance I woke up early one morning, wrapped a towel around me and headed for the shower. I was going to the gym and I always like to shower before and after. Everyone else was asleep, or so I thought.

As I walked down the passage towards the shower, which was in the laundry along with our second toilet, I caught a glimpse of someone in the kitchen. It was a peripheral-vision thing. When I turned to look there was no one there, just the early-morning sun coming through the venetian blinds.

Once I was dressed I grabbed my sports bag and went to get my car keys from the glass bowl on my dresser, where I always put them. They weren't there.

I searched the floor, then the clothes I'd had on the previous night. No keys. Next I went into the kitchen – not there. I was starting to get worried. I only had the one set, with my house keys, the key to the gym and the ignition key for my old bomb.

I was standing there trying to figure out where on earth I had put the damn things when Alison went past on her way to the bathroom. I asked her if she had seen them. She just shook her head. I was about to get on the phone and call my training buddy to come and get me when Alison came out of the bathroom and handed me my keys.

'You left them in the handbasin,' she said.

I stood there puzzled. I hadn't been in the bathroom for days. I always used the laundry. The only time I ever had a bath was when I had my rugby aches and pains or my back played up. I always preferred the shower. My razor was at my locker at the gym. I never even used the toilet off the bathroom. It was sort of an unwritten family law: Mum, Alison and guests used the bathroom toilet; fellas used the laundry one.

Puzzled, I headed for the car and my usual day of training and work. When I returned home after rugby practice it was about 8 o'clock at night. The rest of the family were in the lounge watching television.

Mum had my dinner in the warmer. I sat down to eat and as I did so, someone walked past the kitchen door, heading for the laundry. I didn't really see them, it was just a movement. I thought it must be Dad going to the toilet.

I finished my meal, rinsed the dishes and put them in the dishwasher. I decided to watch some telly, but first I wanted to go to the toilet. I knew Dad must still be there because I hadn't seen him come back past the kitchen. My only alternative was to go to the bathroom.

As I walked past the lounge I glanced in to see what was on the box. Imagine my surprise when I saw that the whole family was there. I turned around and went down to the laundry toilet. No one there.

I didn't say anything to anyone: just put it down to imagination. A programme came on that I wanted to see and eventually the others all headed for bed, leaving me alone in the lounge.

The house settled down and I was enjoying my show. At some point I had the feeling I wasn't alone. I turned around and saw a movement at the door. I figured Alison or my brother Tim had paused there to watch the telly for a second on their way past. I had the same sensation a little later.

In the morning I was first up again. It wasn't training this morning, but my shift at the works was doing overtime with an early start. I made toast and coffee and I noticed that there was a lipstick on the bench. It was Mum's colour so I assumed it was hers – but it was odd because, as I have said, Mum is a stickler for neatness. Everything has a place, and lipstick did not live on the bench. I sort of had a chuckle to myself, left it there and took off. Days later, when we catalogued what had been happening, Mum swore she had not left the lipstick there.

Other little things I noticed in the days that followed included earrings and other pieces of jewellery sitting in funny places. My car keys vanished from the bowl in the room and appeared on the coffee table in the lounge. Tim, who was still at school, didn't have a car yet, but he had a 50cc putt-putt. He went frantic one day looking for his keys, which normally hung on the board by the front door. Mum ran him to school that day, and later found the keys sitting on the washing machine. Alison lost her favourite pendant, one that Suzy had given her. It was found in the bath. As for me, more and more I had that corner-of-the-eye impression that someone had just walked by, vanishing around the bend in the hall, or around the door frame.

Eventually someone mentioned something and we started comparing notes. It turned out everyone in the family had seen (or not seen) the figure who was almost there. In fact, Tim had walked into my room one night and asked me what I wanted. I looked at him blankly. I was lying in bed reading.

'What do you mean?' I asked.

'Didn't you just walk out of my room?' he asked. He'd been in the lounge. I told him I hadn't been anywhere. He muttered something about Alison and left again. I didn't tell him that Alison was, as usual, in the bathroom and had been for ages.

Proof that something was not right came home to us a few days later. Dad worked at the freezing works as well, as a meat inspector. This particular day a Maori guy who worked on one of the chains came up to Dad at smoko. The man's name was George. Dad didn't really know him, but like a lot of the guys, they were nodding acquaintances. The works was a big place with some two or three hundred people in it.

Anyway, George came up to Dad and said, 'You have been having some strange things happening at your place.' It was a statement not a question and Dad was a bit flabbergasted. He nodded, and asked George how he knew.

'The reason I know is standing right behind you,' came George's reply.

Dad turned but there was no one there.

George sort of chuckled. 'It's a girl. Blonde, but a Maori. I know her name. It's Suzy. She died about a month ago.'

'You can see her?' said Dad.

George nodded. 'Yes. She has been following you every day. I thought she would move on, but she hasn't.'

Dad is not a superstitious person and he really didn't know what to make of this. All he knew was that strange things had been happening and there had to be an explanation. Now here was someone he hardly knew telling him that the ghost of a dead girl was following him around, and had been for several weeks.

'I can help you,' George went on. 'I'm holding a healing hui in a few weeks up at the marae. If you and your family come up I'll be able to sort things out for you. I'll tell you the day and time nearer. Okay?'

Dad agreed, and told us all about it that night.

Over the next month the strange things kept on happening. Nothing serious, just involving things being moved to where they shouldn't have been. It was always small things, like keys and jewellery. It was as if Suzy's spirit were playing jokes on us. The movements caught out of the corner of the eye also continued.

George told Dad we were to go to the marae on a particular Saturday at 11. Dad had to work, but George said that was okay as long as the rest of the family went. We were to wear tracksuits or trousers – no skirts for the women. It all sounded a bit strange.

At the appointed time Mum, Alison, my brother Tim and I went up to the marae and we were met by George, whom I recognised from the works. There were a lot of people around at the time. The hui was an important one. George took us into the big house, which was quite crowded. Down the back, a screen had been erected to shut an area off from the rest. He took us behind the screen.

The only things we saw there were a massage table and a bowl of water on the floor beside it. George told us to sit down on the floor, which we did. He went out for a minute, then came back with a woman. She was young, in her early twenties. George introduced her as his daughter Nancy.

'Could you please take off your shoes and lie on the table, face down?' George asked Alison. It became plain then why he had asked us, or Mum and Alison, to wear trackies or similar. Alison was nervous but she did what he asked.

As she lay there, George drew Alison's arms out in front of her and Nancy came and took hold of her hands. George then went to Alison's feet and began to massage her. He slowly worked his way up her body. As he did so, he chanted in Maori. I speak Maori but I didn't understand much of what he was saying. It was like a different language or dialect.

As George worked his way up Alison's back, Alison began to shake and her hands and arms were quivering and jerking. Nancy was having difficulty hanging on to Alison's hands and George's voice was getting more and more urgent.

It was when George got to Alison's shoulders that her hands and arms suddenly went limp. He stopped the massage and straightened up. He looked tired.

'Okay. That's the first stage,' he said, then, looking at me, 'You are the strong one. He might be too strong for you,' he added, looking at Nancy, 'but we will see.' It was just about this time that I became aware that my old back injury had decided to flare up.

'Is Suzy here?' I asked. George nodded.

'Oh yes, she's here, 'she's sitting on your feet,' he replied. That was not quite what I'd expected to hear.

'You're next,' he said. As I started to get up he held up his hand.

'Stay where you are.'

George came over to where I was sitting, bringing the bowl of water with him. Nancy came and knelt in front of me, while George stood behind me. My back was hurting like hell by now and I wondered what effect his massage would have on me.

It came as a shock when instead of massaging me as he had done with Alison, all George did was start dipping his fingers in the bowl of water and trickling it across my neck. At the same time he began chanting again, and phrases I understood were about 'leaving' and 'it is time to move on'.

My back got worse and my hands and arms started to shake just as Alison's had. I couldn't control them. Nancy, who was holding my hands, was fighting to stop losing her grip. She did let one hand go. George caught it and held it until she could grab it again.

'Too strong,' said Nancy. 'Too strong for me.'

George called out, and another woman came in from the big room. This woman was probably in her thirties. She was dressed in black with a shawl over her shoulders. She changed places with Nancy, who left.

We started again. George was still just dripping the water on the back of my neck and chanting and talking. The woman holding my hands had to fight to keep her grip as my hands and arms started to shake. She was very strong. Remember, at that time I was heavily into weight training and I could bench-press some pretty impressive numbers, but somehow she hung on. George's voice was really urgent, the water was soaking my shirt and my back was on fire. It had never been this bad before.

Then the woman in black who was holding my hands started to talk. It was English, but it sounded strange. Her words came in bursts and gasps.

'It's so black,' she said, 'so cold and black.'

Then she was shaking her head.

'No I won't,' she said.

This went on and the pain in my back just got worse and worse. I was just about yelling myself. The woman's nails were digging in to my hands. This couldn't be right.

Then suddenly the pain in my back was gone and a new sensation started. A delicious heat started right at my tailbone and flowed up my spine. It was a burning sensation that just blew the pain away. It came rolling up, and when it got to my neck it flowed sideways into my shoulders, and from there it moved down my arms. My arms and hands were no longer shaking. I felt the heat pass from me to the woman in black, and then it was over. I had no more pain. I also, for a few seconds, had no strength. The woman let my hands go and they just fell. I was exhausted.

'It's done,' said George, sitting back. 'She's moved on.' The woman in black got to her feet and left without a word.

'What has just happened?' I looked at George for an explanation.

'Later,' he said. 'I have a very busy day ahead of me. Come and talk to me at lunchtime Monday and I'll tell you more.'

With that, we all went home to a house that never again had strange things happen in it. I saw George on the Monday and he explained what had happened and why. In a nutshell, it went like this.

Suzy had developed a real attachment to, a love, even, for our family. We were the family she wanted to belong to; our home was the home she wanted to live in. When she was killed so suddenly and so violently her spirit attached itself to us, and in particular to Alison.

George explained that it was as if Suzy's spirit were attached to Alison by an umbilical cord. The cord could be stretched to infinity. She would follow Dad to work, Alison to school, me to the gym. Moving things around the house was her way of saying that she was here and that she loved us and that she was frustrated that we couldn't see her. She didn't necessarily know that she was dead, just that things had changed.

What George had done that day at the marae was select me for my strength, and invite and persuade Suzy's spirit to leave Alison and attach itself to me, which it did. Then he had used his powers to drive it from me and send it on its way. The reason he had done this exorcism on me rather than on Alison was because he had been scared that harm could have been done to her under the stress of the exercise, whereas there was less risk with me because I was stronger physically.

As a footnote, George and I became very good friends. In many ways he has become my mentor, my teacher. I am learning much from him. Shortly we will be conducting healing sessions together.

The Patu

Finders should not always be keepers. The events in this story took place only a few years ago. The young man at the centre of it is now 25, and he still awakes some nights with his heart pounding and the realisation that the is lucky to be alive.

It was a hot summer and my brother David, best friend Steve and my tag-along sister Susan were doing what we normally did during our summer holidays at the crib. We explored the headland and its caves and played in the sand dunes. Generally we managed a fair slice of both of these on any given day, along with some swimming, mussel-gathering and fishing.

I was the big boy at the time, 13 years old and pretty crabby with the onset of puberty. The others were all within a couple of years of me, except for Susan, who was only nine. I resented the fact that Mum and Dad made me responsible for looking after her. But there were no kids close to her age so I – we – were stuck with her. In a way my resentment contributed to what happened.

We were playing hide and seek one day in the sand dunes. Basically it was a game in which we, the boys, would run away and hide from Susan, and if we were lucky we wouldn't see her for an hour or two.

We're talking big sand dunes here. They were probably 50 feet high at their highest point and they were maybe a mile long, running from headland to headland the length of the bay. They were deep as well: in some places there would be up to seven or eight big waves of dunes before the lupins started, then the pine trees that separated the sand from the holiday camp and farms beyond.

This day David, Steve and I did what we normally did. 'You're it!' someone screamed at Susan and we three boys sprinted away in all directions. Susan shouted, 'Not fair!' as she always did, and started running after David, who was the slowest.

I took off to the far end of the beach, where the sand hills and the cliff were separated by a small tidal creek when the entrance to the sea was open. But today the entrance was closed and the water in the creek was brown and warm. I paddled down the edge so I didn't leave any footprints.

There was a place above the creek where the sand formed its own cliff – the wind blowing up the creek from the sea must have carved it. Anyway,

THE PATU

in this sort of cliff face there were a couple of deep cracks, or crevices. They extended from the top for several feet, and were filled with silver tussock. I figured this was the perfect place to hide.

I climbed up onto one end of this sand dune, then walked along the top and dropped into one of the crevices. Down in the bottom I lay in the tussock grass and wormed my way forward so I could see down the creek towards the beach and the sea.

I saw Susan go across my line of vision, then nothing. I suppose I got a bit bored. Staying hidden from Susan wasn't really much of a challenge. I sat up and had a good look around me. The open-ended hole I was sitting in went back about six or seven feet into the sand hill. Looking up, I guessed I was about the same distance below the surface.

You the reader will already have conjured up the word 'grave'. To me, that word wasn't to come until much later. I was just a kid doing kid stuff. Anyway it was as I wriggled around that I hit my knee on something hard. It hurt but I didn't cry or anything – I was a big boy.

I had a bit of a scrabble around in the hard sand at the bottom of the hole to see what I had hit. There, mostly buried beneath the surface of the sand, was a mere.* I knew what a mere was. I had seen them in the museum and in books and on television. Mostly they were shown as greenstone or polished wood but this one was different. It was made of white – or rather yellow – stuff that I guess was some sort of bone. Whale bone perhaps. Whatever bone it was, it must have been a big one.

I wiped all the sand off the mere and moved back to the entrance of my hole to where the light was better. There I had a decent look. There was some carving on the handle, but this mere wasn't a real fancy one like a lot of the ones I had seen in pictures. I remember thinking that this one was for serious work. I had a pretty good idea of how they worked – sort of like a knife when you cut the top off a boiled egg. Only the egg was the skull of the person you were fighting.

I took a couple of swings with it. It was quite heavy and I could imagine it would be pretty dangerous.

This was cool. There was no question that I would keep the mere. In my mind that was fair enough. I'd found it, therefore it was mine. At 13 life is pretty straightforward.

I had a few more swings, then I put the mere to one side and decided to see if there was anything else here that I could find to take home. Our

---

* The object Troy found was, in fact, a patu not a mere. A mere is made of greenstone; a patu of whale bone.

holiday was just about over and a few mementoes were just what I needed.

I had a good poke around but couldn't find anything, just some old bones – probably a dog or pig or whatever – it still hadn't crossed my mind that I was sitting in the bottom of a grave.

I decided to go and show the others what I had found. It was too steep and the sand was too soft for me to climb back up the sides of the hole, so I decided to drop out the end and slide down to the creek. No problem. I was probably 20 feet up but I'd been hurtling down steep sand slides for the last two weeks.

I pushed the mere down into the back of my pants and prepared myself for a short fast ride. I pushed off and away I went. The drop was almost vertical, and I landed safely on my feet and bum on a little ridge of soft sand at the bottom. Great stuff, I was thinking and was just standing up to go when the sky went dark. That's the last thing I remember.

Much later I found out what had happened. At the time of my slide a whole section of the sand cliff had detached itself and fallen, burying me. By some miracle my father, uncle and another family friend were out looking for us to take us fishing and my uncle saw the whole incident happen in front of him.

I was dug out alive from under four feet of sand. I was unconscious and my airways were blocked with sand. I was revived and spent two days in hospital, suffering breathing problems and severe bruising.

The weird thing is that when I was dragged from the sand, my rescuers didn't notice any mere. It wasn't in my trousers or anywhere that they could see – of course they didn't know of its existence and I wasn't up to telling them.

I recovered fully from my adventure and I've been back to that place a few times since, but I've never been down that part of the creek again. I don't regard myself as particularly superstitious but today, 12 years later, I concede that there is something to be understood here.

I do believe that my actions in attempting to take what I now know was a burial relic from a Maori grave site started something more than just a sand slide.

I came as close to death as anyone and survived. I have nightmares still, and in them I see that mere. They are definitely not pleasant for me or my partner.

The Cave

We have been careful to ensure that real locations and people are not compromised in this collection of stories, partly to protect individuals but also to preserve places that are sacred to Maori and/or physically sensitive. This story was told to me by a friend who is a keen yachtsman and diver.

It was in the late 1980s when I had my one and only experience that you could consider an encounter with the spirit world.

There were four of us aboard my yacht *Sea Wasp*. It was summer and we were on an extended three-week cruise in one of New Zealand's most picturesque boating areas. It had been a leisurely, fun experience. We cruised slowly under sail most of the time, mooring and picnicking in some stunningly beautiful places, and fishing and diving for the bulk of our food as we went.

It was a cruise of exploration and discovery, as it turned out, in more ways than one. None of us had sailed these particular waters before. Every bay, every island was a fresh and welcome experience. There were a few other boats around and groups of shore-based campers, but there was never a crowd. It was perfect.

My brother Ted and I were the divers and anglers and spent a lot of time messing about in the rubber ducky. Our wives, Sally and Pat, were content to swim, sunbathe and explore the shore and islands on foot, or just laze around with a glass of wine and a book.

One day the yacht was snug in a sheltered mooring and the girls had swum to the beach to sunbathe and go for a walk. Ted and I had dropped their gear and refreshments on the beach for them and taken the runabout to go for a dive off a steep headland. We figured the deep water and a possible underwater cliff face would be prime crayfish territory.

We were right. This initial visit was an exploratory one. We had left the tanks on the boat being recharged by our little compressor and we were equipped with just snorkel gear. But we didn't need the tanks. There were crays aplenty only a few feet down and we soon had a half dozen each. There would be crayfish barbecued with garlic butter for dinner and we'd boil the rest for a cray and salad lunch the following day as we cruised on.

We put our loaded dive bags into the boat, which we had tied off to a rock. The tide was going out so the rubber ducky was being held well out of harm's way. The sea was calm, there was no wind and the sun was bright. A perfect day.

'Let's just cruise for a while,' Ted suggested. 'Might pick up a nice fish.' He took his speargun, I grabbed an empty dive bag and we set off finning along the face of the cliff.

The face dropped away steeply below us and the water was crystal clear. As we cruised along we could see the antennae of dozens of crays protruding out from crevices and under ledges. The place was swarming with them. There were plenty of fish as well – big trevally and blue cod feeding in the kelp that fringed the tide.

Ted nailed a fat trevally and tied it to his belt. A little later he got the biggest bluey I have ever seen. While Ted was playing the great white hunter I found a patch of big paua and took a half dozen, then added a dozen big plump mussels. I could visualise paua fritters followed by a beaut paella with mussels, crayfish and cod. It was hard not to scavenge for food in this place. There was definitely no shortage of supply. We weren't there to rape and pillage, just taking what we needed. I reckon in only 20 minutes in the water we had enough tucker for the next two days.

We swam on and then we came to a cave. It was low to the water. The tide was full out at that stage but there was just a couple of feet of the entrance showing above the water. Underwater, the opening extended maybe 10 feet down. My first thought was octopus – not a denizen of the deep, rather a nice little fella to finish the paella. I've spent a lot of time in the Greek Islands and I know a trick or three to turn the potentially rubbery beasts into the perfect addition to my famous dish.

'Let's bring the boat up,' I suggested. 'There's a torch in the kit.'

'Yeah, why not,' replied Ted.

We swam the hundred yards back around the cliff and zipped back in the runabout. The tide was flat so we wedged the sand anchor into a crevice in the rock to hold the dinghy safely while we went exploring.

I led with the torch. Ted reloaded his speargun just in case we encountered an unfriendly inhabitant, and we swam in. After about five feet the roof climbed away above us. The water was perhaps 10 feet deep, but shallowed quite rapidly.

There were no nasties there apart from a moray who snarled at us from the safety of his cave within the cave. We ignored him. There were quite a few fish including a big snapper that shot out like a rocket.

I pushed my mask back and treaded water, using the torch to gauge the size of the cave. The air was fine. The place was big, probably the size of

THE CAVE

the average Kiwi house. There was some beach of coarse sand covered in the usual rubbish – seaweed, plastic bottles and pieces of polystyrene. The only thing of any relative value was a glass fishing float. I kicked over to grab it before Ted saw it.

I stood up on the beach and Ted joined me. 'Reminds me of my cellar,' he muttered. 'About as damp as well.'

I swept the torch around. Above the beach there was jumble of fallen rock and behind that what seemed to be a wide ledge. I pulled my fins off and gingerly climbed up.

The ledge was above the tide line by maybe five or six feet. It ran the width of the cave and was maybe 10 or 12 feet at its widest point. There were some rocks on it that had obviously fallen from the roof and walls over the years, but for the most part the surface was flat.

'Give me some light,' Ted called and I turned and lit the way so he could scramble up to where I was. As he sat there I went exploring.

The back wall of the cave that came down to the ledge was full of crevices and holes. There were signs that birds and maybe bats lived or had lived here at some time, judging by the crude nests and the droppings. While Ted remained in the dark, I carried on poking the light into every hole and crack in the rock. I have no idea what I was looking for, but when I found it, my heart just about jumped out of my mouth.

The skull was in an indentation in the rock at one end of the ledge. As in all good pirate and treasure stories, it was grinning at me. It wasn't white – more yellow or light brown. And the rest of the skeleton was there as well.

'Come and look at this!' I called back at Ted and he came stumbling along the ledge, calling for me to give him some light. but I couldn't move my arm. Maybe I was gripped by a childish fear that the skeleton would get up and grab me.

'Shit!' was all Ted managed to get out when he finally got to me. 'Shipwreck,' he ventured.

'No, mate,' I replied.

While he'd been coming along the ledge I'd had a bit more time to check out what I'd found. The skeleton had been undisturbed by birds or rats or anything else and obviously the tide didn't get this high. It lay flat in the bottom of the niche it was in, stretched out full length. It was half covered with something that I thought was a cloth, but when I peered more closely I could see it was made of feathers – a cloak.

Lying across the chest area was a long wooden spear or club. I don't know the Maori name for it, but it is the one with the fake spearhead and the wide flat blade. The bones of one hand were resting on it. The arm bones had long since separated and were lying beside the remains. There was some flax cord and a greenstone chisel or ornament where the neck bones were. The bones had all separated after the body had decayed but they all lay in position so it was plain to see every detail.

'I think we'd better leave, mate,' Ted was saying and I couldn't have agreed more. Whoever the body had been, he – it – had been laid out in this place by someone. It hadn't got here by itself. I don't know much Maori lore but I know that burial places are considered sacred and that many of them have a curse or tapu put on them. I was as keen as Ted to get out of the cave.

We turned and made our way back down the ledge, pulled on our fins and made for the cave mouth. Once on board the boat we pulled off our head gear and breathed a joint sigh of relief.

'Boy, going exploring with you is pretty weird!' Ted was muttering as he unzipped his wetsuit. I started the motor and we pulled away. It was only as we were moving that I noticed a dinghy standing about 50 feet off the cliff.

There were three guys in it, all of them Maori. One of them was waving at us. I turned towards them and killed the engine. We drifted up to the other boat and one of the men reached out and grabbed the side rope to hold us against them.

'You guys came out of there pretty fast,' one of them said.

'You bet,' I replied. 'I didn't think that was a good place to hang about in.'

The guy nodded. 'You got that right, mate. You touch anything?'

'No way,' I said, remembering I'd left the fishing float behind. I wasn't going back to get it.

'Good!' the speaker was saying. 'It's a sacred place. We were fishing and we saw you go in. Thought we'd better come and have a chat.'

One of the other guys opened a chillybin and pulled out some cans of beer. He handed them around, and one each to Ted and me, so I figured we weren't in too much trouble.

'What's the story?' I asked as we sat there on the tide. 'Once we saw the skeleton we decided that it wasn't the place for us.'

'Not the place for anyone, Pakeha or Maori,' replied the oldest man in the other boat.

We sat there for half an hour as the tide changed and they told us the story of the body in the cave. It all happened more than 200 years ago.

THE CAVE

Maori war parties were fighting in the area. There was a series of battles fought on the water and nearby beaches, with several tribes involved.

One tribe lost their chief and, seriously outnumbered, they were forced to flee. They took the body of the chief with them as they tried to fight their way to safety. But they were cornered, and decided to hide the body to prevent their enemies from cutting its head off and desecrating the body.

One of the warriors knew of the cave from food-gathering expeditions in the peaceful past. The decision was made to hide their chief's body there. They would escape and come back for him later to give him a proper burial.

One group of warriors took a waka and raced away from the other canoes, leaving their fellows to delay their pursuers. As soon as they were safely out of sight around the headland, they paddled to the cave. There, some of them took the body and swam into the cave, where they laid their chief in his temporary resting place. The tide was high – over the cave entrance – when they swam out and got back on board their war canoe. They then went to rejoin the battle.

They and the others were killed or captured to be eaten or become slaves. The secret of what they had done with their chief was passed on down through the years by those who had survived as slaves. The remaining members of the tribe, who had to flee their home land in the wars that followed, made the decision to leave the body where it had been laid. Since then the cave has been tapu.

'We keep an eye on it,' the old man said.

'Will the tapu affect us?' asked Ted, a worried look on his face. I must admit I was a bit anxious as well.

The old man shook his head. 'If you didn't touch anything you'll be okay. If you took anything with you, you would take the tapu as well and that wouldn't be good.'

I had the feeling that this was a slight understatement but I kept quiet. I'm not a particularly superstitious person but I wasn't about to test the water on that one.

'We must go and fish,' the old man said finally. 'Don't tell anyone what you have found. The dead deserve to be left in peace.'

'Amen to that,' Ted muttered. 'Don't worry, we won't say a word.'

'Good,' came the reply.

The crays in the bag by my feet were kicking. I opened the bag and tipped them out into the bottom of the boat. 'You guys want a cray or two?' I asked.

'Oh yeah!' one of the younger ones was grinning at me.

I passed over half of what we had. We'd get some more before we sailed in the morning.

The trio in the dinghy thanked us, started their outboard and cruised away with a wave, heading away from the cliff. Ted and I headed back to our boat. I noticed that the dinghy went about a half mile out and stopped. I couldn't help feeling that the men in it were not just fishing. I think they and their people probably kept an eye on all the traffic on the water, particularly during the summer months, to ensure that the cave was not desecrated.

'No word to anyone,' I said to Ted as we headed past the yacht towards where the girls were waiting on the beach.

'You better believe it, brother,' he said.

I never mentioned the cave for years and when I did, I never gave anyone the faintest clue where it was. I still won't.

We finished our cruise that summer without any further incident. We all agreed that it was the holiday of a lifetime. I'm planning on repeating it some day soon, and I have the feeling that when I do, and I'm in the area where the cave is, there will be a dinghy with a few Maori blokes in it anchored not far away.

The Old Lady

The events in this story set a friend of mine to thinking very deeply about what the eyes can and can't see, and what unseen things surround us.

A piece of Maori carving or whakairo that was very important to my people was coming to the museum in our nearby town. This heirloom had been created by an ancestor and over the years it had passed through many hands, ending up far away from our tribal lands.

Now the beautiful wooden whakairo was being returned home to a place of honour in the museum, on display for all to see and enjoy. Our people were pleased about this. It was such a wonderful work that it deserved to be appreciated by everyone.

Members of my family decided that it was important that they go and see the whakairo, greet its return, and pay their respects to the spirit of the man who had created it. The old people felt it was particularly important for the youngsters to be involved so that they would have a greater appreciation of their heritage.

I wasn't there when this incident happened but I have been told the story by those who were. My mother, her sister Nina, my niece Ricki and Ricki's son Billy, who was about five at the time, set off to town in Nina's car.

At the museum the party went to view the work of our ancestor. They spent quite a lot of time there before wandering off among the other exhibits. So involved were they that it came as a surprise when they realised how late in the day it was. Billy was complaining of hunger and the women decided it was definitely time for a cup of tea.

The four of them walked to the car and were about to get in when Billy asked suddenly, 'Is the old lady coming with us?' All three women looked at him to see if he was joking. He wasn't. Billy could be a pretty serious five-year-old and he was being serious.

'What old lady?' asked Ricki.

'The old lady from the museum. She was with us all the way around there and now she's sitting next to me.' Billy was by now sitting in the back seat. There was a space between himself and his mother.

'She's got a moko like Aunty Reni,' he said.

Aunty Reni was his great-aunt. She was very old, close to 100, and she had a moko on her chin.

The three women all sat looking at one another for a moment or two longer, not knowing what to say. Eventually Nina started the car and headed out of town. Her passengers sat there in silence. Even Billy, who was normally pretty vocal, didn't say anything more, until they turned off the motorway and started down the side-road towards home.

'She wants out here,' Billy suddenly piped up.

Nina stopped the car – quite quickly, Ricki told me. Billy opened the back door, got out, waited a moment, waved, then got back into the car and Nina drove on. Mum has since showed me where they stopped. It was close to an old pa and burial site.

The women didn't say anything about their mysterious passenger until Billy had grabbed a sandwich and gone off to play with the other kids. It was Nina who spoke first. None of them, it seems, had doubted for a moment that what Billy had seen was real.

'She just wanted to see the whakairo, same as we did,' said Nina. 'It's a long way from town. Maybe she got a lift in as well.'

'Why did Billy see her but we didn't?' Ricki asked.

It was mother who had the answer to that one. 'Sometimes children see things as they are, while we see them as we think they are, or as we want them to be.'

Neither Mother, Nina nor Ricki have ever had any doubts since that Billy saw what he saw and was telling the truth. He never mentioned the old lady again.

People Who See

There can be no doubt that some people see things, while others don't. When a friend asked a group of such people why they saw things that others remained blind to, one replied 'If you don't believe, then you don't see.' This is not so much a story, as an observation passed on to me by my friend.

I am a Maori, more new school than old perhaps, but I am proud of who I am and where I come from. I speak the language fluently, take pride in my knowledge of our traditions and our history. I participate in many of our cultural events and I hope, represent my people well. I try to anyway. Yet, I can't see what some of the others can. Perhaps I am glad that I can't.

There are people I know who have experiences that many of us, Maori and Pakeha, would find hard to live with. These people see those who have gone before. They don't see them as visions or ghosts - those semi-transparent figures of popular mythology. No, their ghosts are as solid as you or me.

It all seems so normal, so ordinary to people with the ability to see. Those with the vision might be out walking and be joined by a ghost, or a Jimmy, as we call them. They might be driving and see a dead relative or friend standing at the side of the road. They will stop and pick them up, take them where they want to go, enjoy a korero (talk) with them.

There may be questions about the family, who is well and unwell, who is getting married, who is expecting a child – the usual questions that friends and family ask of one another. Sometimes there may be a word of warning.

In the far north, at Rerenga Wairua (Farewell Spit), the spirits of the dead have been seen walking the beaches to their place of departure to their new world. Children in times not so long ago used to play with these departing spirits, which they (and adults with the sight) could see plainly. The spirits always responded to the children and returned their play in kind, with good nature and laughter, until it was time for them to move on to the point, and wait to dive into the waves that would carry them home. People with 'the sight' can still see the spirits at Rerenga Wairua today.

Children often have the ability to see what is not visible to the eyes of adults. Are a child's 'secret friends' more than just figments of their imagination?

'You must believe in order to see.' Those were the words one of those people offered to me when I asked her 'Why can't I see what you see?' I know this woman well, she is my aunt, and she has always had this ability – or this curse, some might say.

Do I want to be able to see the way she does? I really don't know. I find my life is complicated enough as it is without having visions from my past appearing in front of my eyes, talking to me, joking with me. Then again, there are people from my past I would like to exchange words with, words that were never said when we were all alive together.

The Smell of Death

Like many people whose stories are told on these pages, Aaron's experience with the supernatural or unknown was one single incident in a lifetime. He was living in the Far North at the time.

I was home from the army for recuperation at the time this thing happened. I had been injured in a training accident – a truck smash. Nothing really serious, just a broken wrist and some bruises, but they sent me home for a few weeks. I was to go back when my plaster came off.

It was good for me: a bit of a holiday, a chance to catch up with some of my old mates and a girlfriend or two.

I arrived home on a Friday afternoon, having driven all the way up from Waiouru in the old Holden. My mother and father were home, along with one of my sisters. My other two brothers and sister were married and living all around the district. Mum and Dad were putting on a big do on the Sunday so we could all get together. Dad and I and his best mate Alby were going to put down a hangi.

'We'll go fishing tomorrow,' Dad told me on the Friday night. 'Your Uncle Hepi has a big pig waiting. Irikori [my brother] and Moana [his wife] are getting mussels and pipi and kina. It's going to be a good feed!'

Dad was full of enthusiasm. He loved his tucker and he loved getting the family together, especially for a celebration rather than a tangi, which was happening more and more often with the people of his generation.

Next day Dad and Alby and I went out in Dad's dinghy to set a couple of nets, then we were going to go out to our secret grouper hole to line-fish for a couple of big ones. A cousin down the coast was getting us some koura (crayfish) as well. I love crays, they are a real favourite of mine.

The sea was calm when we went out. We set two nets to catch moki, tarakihi, maybe trevally. That's always the great thing about fishing, you never know exactly what you're going to get. We left the nets in the shallows and went out to the reef to find the grouper hole. Dad lined up his markers and Alby dropped the anchor onto the reef itself, letting us drift out so we were sitting right where he wanted us to be.

With the outboard off the old guys started talking. The big topic at the time was the father of my friend Norm. Denny had gone fishing two weeks before, alone in his little wooden dinghy. He hadn't come back that night, and no one had seen him since. His boat hadn't been found and nothing had been washed up on the beaches. That was the worst of it for our people, particularly the older ones. Everyone knew that old Denny was dead, but without the body, things couldn't be laid to rest.

'I reckon it was here,' Dad was saying. 'He always came to fish for hapuka, that was his favourite fish.'

'But why didn't he come ashore? And what happened to his boat? Even broken it would float,' replied Alby. I just kept quiet and concentrated on willing a big fat hapuka onto my hook.

Alby caught a nice one that would have weighed in at 15 pounds. Then I hooked something big. We were using hand lines, the thick linen cod ones. I don't know what the breaking strain is on them, but it is pretty heavy.

Whatever I had hooked into was big. It was fighting, but it was a strange sluggish action.

'Big one, boy!' Dad was saying. He and Alby pulled their lines up so as not to snag me. I was hauling big time for maybe 10 minutes. I couldn't figure it out – I didn't have that much line out, but it seemed to be stretching or something.

Then Alby let out a yell. 'Hey, Aaron! You've got a rope on there!'

I think right about then we all knew what we had, but no one actually said it. When my hook brought the rope in close enough, Dad and Alby grabbed it. I pulled my hooks off and we started to haul up the rope. It was a half-inch hemp rope, an anchor rope, and it was caught at both ends. We all got a hand on it and pulled so hard that our little dinghy was in danger of going under. Then finally something gave. The end of the rope furthest from the reef started to move. It was heavy though, really heavy.

I think we were all feeling pretty apprehensive. I mean, we all knew what we were probably going to find when we pulled up the weight at the end of the rope. But it still came as a huge shock.

Poor old Denny didn't look the best after two weeks down there. The anchor rope had wound itself around his waist somehow, maybe when his old boat had tipped.

Denny's dinghy was hovering below him in the water. I had no idea what could have made a wooden dinghy sink. Maybe Denny's dead weight and the outboard, maybe water pressure, whatever.

'Cut the rope to the boat,' Dad told Alby. Dad's little boat was pretty heavy in the water because of the weight, and the sea was coming up.

'No, leave him in the water,' I said. 'We'll tow him to the beach.' It was the most practical way. Denny's body was very bloated and the boat was only an eight- or nine-footer.

We cut the rope at the anchor end, tied it to one of the carry handles in the stern and slowly started back for the beach. Alby tossed the big hapuka he'd caught over the side. 'Wouldn't be right,' he said, and Dad and I had to agree.

Well, we didn't go ahead with the hangi as such. Instead, all the food and everything was used for Denny's official farewell. I didn't mind. I was just pleased for my mate Norm. At least he had his Dad back for the ceremonies and that was important to him.

When Denny was buried I was a couple of days off getting my plaster off and going back to camp. Norm and I and a few of the others had a bit of a night at the pub on the last Saturday night.

I was sleeping in the whare out the back of the house, which had been built for us boys years before. It was two bedrooms at either end and a sort of living room in the middle that we used to use as a party room.

At the moment I was alone in the place. During Denny's tangi my brothers had been there with me, but they had gone back home.

Late that night I crashed into bed, going out like a light.

I have no idea what time I woke up, but it was still dark outside. What woke me was the smell. It's a smell that once you've been exposed to it, you never forget. It was the smell of decaying flesh – human flesh.

As a professional soldier I had been involved in search and rescue and other incidents. I had seen (and smelt) bodies in many states. Denny's body hadn't been the worst of them.

But now, in the dark, I was sitting up in my bed gagging from the unexpected smell and its closeness. There was no light but I could see a shape standing in the doorway. It was a big figure – very tall, very fat. It just stood there and sort of glowed white-green. I couldn't see any features, just the shape.

I couldn't yell – I couldn't even whisper: my throat was closed, my mouth dry. I didn't dare take a deep breath because of the stench. I lifted my sheet and pulled it tight across my nose and mouth.

I don't know how long we stayed like that. Then the figure just raised its right arm, turned and went out through the door.

I sat there in my bed for maybe four or five minutes. When I took the sheet from my nose and mouth the stench of rot was gone from the air, but it was still trapped in my nose and in my mind.

Eventually I got out of bed and went through the whare turning on the lights. There was no one, nothing there apart from me. With my night's sleep well and truly shot I got dressed and went into the house for a much-needed cup of coffee.

I was sitting there drinking it when Dad came in. He looked as bad as I felt. I knew immediately that what had happened to me had also happened to him. When we talked, it was exactly so.

We sat up until the sun rose, then when we saw signs of life across at Alby's place we went across. Alby's hands were shaking as he tried to drink his cup of tea. He had seen the same thing at the same time.

Alby's brother Thad was a tohunga and the three of us went straight around to see him. Thad listened to our collective story. It was the same for each of us: the smell, the figure, the raised hand, everything. Funny thing was that neither Mum nor Alby's wife Alison had woken up.

'He just came to thank you for finding him and bringing him back to his whanau,' said Thad. 'Simple as that. His spirit was saying goodbye and he couldn't leave without thanking you.'

Nothing like that has ever happened to me again. Mind you, I haven't made a habit of recovering the bodies of friends and members of my iwi from the depths. Maybe if I did, I would have that experience more often. I think I'll just leave things where they stand.

Distant Fires

Many of the tales told to me over the 25 or so years I have been collecting them have similarities. This one was told to me by a very elegant woman who is a writer herself.

In 1969 my husband Martin and I took over the management of a farm on a North Island peninsula, a place that since those days has become a holiday centre. The farms are all but gone now. Instead, there are small holdings and baches and holiday homes all over the place.

Back then, before leisure became something of an industry, the peninsula had two farms with sheep and beef cattle. There were no baches, just grassy ridges, bush gullies and patches of original and regenerating native bush. Along the shore on our side of the peninsula there were rocky outcrops separating many small crescents of golden sand with a fringe of pohutukawa above. It was quite beautiful, particularly when the pohutukawa flamed.

The farmhouse sat right dead centre in the bay. The house was probably 100 years old then. Solid, built of heart timber, it nestled among fruit trees with some wonderful specimens of native trees, including kauri.

The house sat on a small rise and the yard gave way to a narrow paddock. Beyond that was the golden sand of the beach that formed the head of the bay. The right arm of the bay was rugged cliff, with only one small beach. On the cliff top there was coarse grazing for another farm that was situated in the next bay.

Looking back, I suppose we were probably isolated by today's standards, but we didn't feel it. It was a full hour's drive over winding shingle roads to get to the nearest store. We had a boat, an old wooden clinker thing fitted with a Ford 10 motor. Often Martin and I and our two children would take the boat and go fishing, or picnic on one of our beaches. There were very few other craft around at that time, except in the summer; even then, compared with today, they were few and far between.

Over the summer months the odd yacht from Auckland or the Bay of Islands would cruise in to overnight or shelter. Often the crew would come ashore and have a picnic or barbecue on one of the beaches.

People were more polite then. Most of the time the yachts would sail right up to our little jetty and tie up, while someone came and asked if it was all right to land. We never refused anyone, just asked that they didn't cut down any growing trees, and that they took their rubbish away with them. I think they all did. We never had any problems for years.

By about 1973 or so there suddenly seemed to be a lot more people and boats around, particularly motorboats. People started coming ashore and camping. Trees were cut down. There was always rubbish left lying around, and frankly, we got sick of it. So we posted signs asking that all visitors call at the farmhouse. It didn't work. Two of the signs were burned on bonfires.

We decided to get nasty – or at least fight back. Martin and Richard, our neighbour, were made official rangers by the local county council. Fortunately, several of the council members were in a similar situation so they were sympathetic. The year before, a group of drunken youths had let a bonfire get out of control and it had destroyed a large amount of bush in a nearby bay.

Permits were now required for overnight camping and fires other than barbecues. Boat names were to be recorded, beaches checked, and boat crews who destroyed trees or littered would be prosecuted by the council.

It was a bit 'police state' in a way, but we had had enough. Several pohutukawa had been cut down; rubbish, including a lot of broken glass, was left lying around, and we lost two sheep that we knew of, their remains found by cooking fires. Richard had lost one calf. It had been roughly butchered and was just a charred mass in a fire pit. They hadn't even eaten it.

Signs went up at the entrance to the bay and every beach was posted as well. That first summer several groups tried it on, but Martin and Richard between them were more than a match for the yahoos. Both of them were big men, and the council had issued them with green shirts and caps and official identification and permit pads and all that sort of stuff. Those people who asked got permits; those who didn't were sent packing.

After that first summer Martin and Richard decided to help campers find firewood because all the standing dead trees near the two favourite beaches had been used. During the winter, every few days Richard would come around in his big boat and the two of them would call in at all the bays on both sides of the peninsula and collect piles of driftwood (and there was always a lot of it). They stacked it up above the high-tide mark.

By summer there were several stacks in each bay and much of it was dry. The summer people were pretty thankful. Of course some idiots set fire to whole piles of wood, but most were good.

I know this is a longwinded story, but it is necessary to set things up so that you can picture the situation as it was back then, and understand why what happened was so bizarre.

It was late summer, almost autumn in fact. Apart from a few groups of fishermen the camping season was over. We'd had no real trouble and breathed a collective sigh of relief that we had our bay back to ourselves. Over the hill Richard and Jane were feeling the same way.

On the Sunday night there were no boats in the bay and no campers on any of the beaches on the peninsula. It was the first time for months we had been alone.

'Peace and quiet at last,' said Martin. We even opened a bottle of wine and took our glasses down to sit on the jetty with our feet dangling over the edge, just watching the sun go down.

It was about midnight when I woke and noticed a flickering glow on the bedroom curtains. Our bedroom was upstairs at the front of the house, with a big dormer window that looked right down the bay. It was a magnificent view during the day.

Tonight, though, all I could see was this dancing light on the sheer curtaining. I jumped out of bed. The threat of fire is bad enough anywhere, but in an isolated place like our bay, and particularly in an old wooden house, it could be devastating.

I pulled open the curtains and breathed a sigh of relief. There certainly were flames, but they weren't near the house. The fire was way down the bay, at the last beach – or the first if you arrive by boat. There was a huge bonfire and my first thought was that all the remaining wood that Martin and Richard had collected had been set alight.

Martin woke up and came to see what I was looking at.

'Damn,' he swore. 'I was hoping that we wouldn't have to do the wood so often this winter. I've got a good mind to go down and give them an earful.'

While I agreed in principle, I didn't want him taking the boat and going all that way by himself at this hour. If there were a few people there and they were drunk it could get nasty. I talked him out of taking the boat and he started considering the other options.

'Can't take the bike down the beach. It's high tide,' he said.

The farm tracks were rough at the best of times but riding the little farm bike over them in the middle of the night wouldn't have been much fun. Our truck was off the road waiting for a new differential so that was out, and the old Vauxhall wasn't cut out for four-wheel driving.

'I'll go down first thing on the bike,' said Martin eventually. Between low tide and half tide there was enough sand to let him ride to the rock that cut the last beach off from its neighbour.

We went back to bed. I woke just in time to see Martin heading out the bedroom door. 'Be careful,' I said, and he was gone.

I heard the bike start up and he was away down the sand. I got up and made a cup of tea and waited. I wasn't really worried but I did say a quiet little prayer. If he wasn't back in an hour I would phone Richard.

It was quite light when I went out onto the front verandah to see what I could see. We had two pairs of old binoculars. One was upstairs on the sill of the bedroom window, the other lived on a little shelf by the verandah door. I focused the glasses and looked down the bay.

The first thing I noticed was that there was no boat moored off the beach. Of course some of the smaller boats could be pulled up on the sand, but I couldn't even see one of those. The tide had turned and was half in again. I could make out Martin's tyre tracks in the sand, and I could see the bike parked by the rocks, but no sign of Martin.

I was puzzled. There wasn't even any smoke from the remains of a bonfire. And it had been high tide when we saw the smoke, so the tide couldn't have extinguished the fire. I went back inside and made another cup of tea. Time was getting on and I was starting to get worried. I was just about to go back out onto the verandah when I heard the sound of the little Honda coming across the paddock out front.

I met Martin at the back door. The first thing that struck me was that he was looking awfully confused.

'What happened?' I asked.

He just shook his head. 'Nothing happened. There was no one there.'

'So what caused the fire?' I wanted to know.

Martin by this time was in the kitchen and pouring himself a cup of tea. 'That's the point,' he said. 'There was no fire.'

'Of course there was,' I replied, becoming a little irritated by all of this. 'We both saw it. It was huge!'

Martin added probably two more spoonfuls of sugar than he normally took as he shook his head.

'Look, I know what *I* saw, I know what *you* saw. But there is no sign of life down there. No boat, no tent, no sign whatsoever of a recent fire. Those two stacks of wood we had down there are still there. A blaze as big as the one we saw would have used a lot of fuel and left a big burn mark. It had to have been above the tide line, but it wasn't. There was nothing there.'

Later that day, when I'd taken the kids up to the top of the hill to catch

DISTANT FIRES

the school bus, I insisted to Martin that we go down to the bay in the boat.

We scrambled all over the area looking for the signs of the fire but to no avail. The only fire signs were a couple of little campfire sites surrounded by rocks, and one place where a small bonfire had been lit. But they were all old. Martin was right: whatever had caused that huge blaze had left no sign, and it had used none of the remaining wood.

We told Richard and Jane about it. Lights from a passing ship or a reflection from the moon was all either of them could offer by way of explanation.

I am a methodical sort of person. I keep a diary, and I have a perpetual calendar on which I mark birthdays and other important events. The day – or rather the night – we saw the fire was 26 February. I noted it in the calendar with the word FIRE in red.

We kept an eye on the beach over the coming months but there were no more fires, and we eventually forgot about it and settled back into our routine.

Eventually, as these things do, the next summer rolled around. There was a bit of trouble this time. The police came in by boat just after New Year looking for some people who had been in a big fight at one of the beach resorts down the coast. A man had been stabbed to death and his killer had been linked to a particular boat.

The presence of the police, even for such a short time, cast quite a pall over the rest of the season. The bad weather came early, and summer was suddenly over.

I remember on 26 February glancing at my perpetual calendar and thinking idly, I wonder if we will see any flames tonight? I even got out of bed and checked twice during the night but there were no flames to be seen.

The next day Martin and I and the kids were off to visit Mum and Dad in Howick. This was to be our holiday. My brother Carl and his wife had come from Tauranga to farm-sit – this was to be their holiday. It was a carefully orchestrated shuffle.

We were away for 10 days. It was nice break, but we were pleased to come home to what we had come to regard as our little corner of the world. Carl and Sue stayed one night with us so we could all catch up. The four of us put the kids to bed and, because it was a mild evening, we went out onto the jetty with our drinks and sat and talked.

As we sat chatting I noticed a fire on the far beach. It was just a little one. I could just make out the riding lights of a yacht at anchor. Carl was sitting beside me and noticed where I was looking.

'It's okay,' he said, 'he came in and I gave him a permit.' Then he added, 'Not like those last ones.'

'What last ones?' I asked.

'The night you left. Someone must have landed there and built a big fire. It was raining like mad but they had a huge fire roaring. Must have used gallons of petrol to keep it going in that downpour.'

I looked across at Martin.

'I was going to go down in the morning and read them the riot act,' Carl continued, 'but when I woke up it was blowing a gale and the boat or whatever it was was gone. You wouldn't have got me out on a boat in that weather.'

'You saw a boat?' Martin asked.

Carl shook his head. 'No. It was pitch black and raining. They had to have had one though – how else could they have got there?' The logic was sound, but Martin just shook his head.

I had been half-expecting in my sub-conscious that the fire thing would repeat on its anniversary. I mean I don't really know what I expected or hoped. But I realised later that while the date may have been right, the measure of the year was probably wrong. I mean, a leap year can throw a date out.

So, given that the fire was back, a year to within a day of when we first saw it, and it was in the pouring rain, where did that leave us? Confused.

We weren't around for the second anniversary of our mysterious fire. Martin got sick later that year and we moved to Auckland to be near the treatment he needed.

Many years later, after Martin had passed on, I was at a dinner party with friends and I was reminiscing about the good times we had had on the peninsula. At some point I mentioned the fire on the beach and how my brother and his wife had seen it almost a year later to the day.

One of the dinner guests was an anthropologist, among other things, and he told us he had an interest in the supernatural or, as he called it, super nature.

'Everything has an explanation,' he said. 'Of course some of the explanations we would rather not consider.' He went on to offer one possible explanation for what Martin and I had experienced.

The professor's theory was that at some time in the past, at that particular time and place, the ancient Maori, or perhaps other peoples, had gathered for a purpose of 'some great significance'. He explained that the whole area had been on the seaborne pathway of many warring tribes over the centuries as they travelled between the north and the East Coast to fight and raid.

'Perhaps the fires were those of victorious warriors who landed to feast on their enemies and celebrate their victory. Perhaps the area has a tapu on it. Will you go back on your special date and look for the fires?' he asked me.

'No,' I said, probably a little more firmly than I intended. 'I think I'm a little too old to go ghost hunting.'

Everyone laughed but underneath it all I couldn't help wondering if he was right, and that the sands of our beautiful beach had once been stained with blood. Perhaps the stains had remained in the stones and the air ever since.

I never went back.

The Uninvited

The woman who told me this tale has vowed that she will never return to the township where the incident took place.

Our family was spread across the South Island, from Christchurch to the West Coast, thanks to my sister and her husband Gordon, who had moved to the coast to live.

Sis's choice of residence made things more inconvenient for Mum than anyone else, but that's the lot of mothers all over the world I guess. Going 'over the hill' to visit them was a major expedition, and one that Mum organised with military precision.

I should explain that Mum was a strict Christian who belonged to a very rigid sect. This all has a bearing on what happened, but it also perhaps helps to show that she was a disciplined person, one who organised herself, and the others in her family, very well.

On this particular occasion Mum went over to the heathen wilderness to bring Christianity to the land, well, at least see her daughter. It was sometimes difficult to tell which was the more important with Mum, God rest her soul.

All joking aside, we loved her dearly, but we were sometimes a little bemused by her religious fervour.

Sis lived in an old railways house. This was not one of those that had been built specifically for the railways, as many had been in that part of the country. Rather, it was a house that had been bought and modernised (that's probably too strong a phrase for it) to be used by railways staff. However, the alterations did include an inside toilet and a new coal range, and the house was warm and comfortable and virtually free, so Sis wasn't complaining.

It was a four-bedroom house and Mum was allocated the back bedroom. This was the first time it had been used in their two months in the place. Sis made the room up for Mum and everyone was looking forward to her visit.

Imagine our surprise when Mum hurried home after just a few days. She was a little out of sorts and we all thought she and Sis must have had a falling out. They had been known to on occasion.

It wasn't that at all: did Mum have a tale to tell us!

THE UNINVITED

The first night she was there, she went to her bedroom at the end of the hall and got into bed, no problem. The bed was warm and comfortable, and she soon began to drop off to sleep.

It was at that very moment that 'something' quite literally jumped on her. She said that she didn't know what it was, but that it was heavy and had very foul breath. We knew (with all due respect) that it couldn't have been Dad, because he was back home in Christchurch with us.

Mum yelled, thrashed about, sat up and turned on the light. There was nothing and no one in the room. Sis and her hubby came flying in to see what was wrong. They said Mum must have had a nightmare, although Mum swore (in the biblical sense) that she hadn't been imagining it.

Being built of stern stuff, and having her very strong faith to hand, she stayed in her bed, and eventually went to sleep.

The next night, when it was time for bed, Mum armed herself. She put her Bible under the pillow and settled down to sleep. Sure enough, just as she was dozing off, the entity came again. She told us that she was rigid with fear, and then she remembered the Bible under her pillow.

She pulled out the good book, told the 'thing' that was lying on her to 'go away, in the name of the Lord!' and, with a terrible keening sound, it went. When she put the light on there was nothing there.

Mum spent the rest of the night lying in her bed reading from her Bible. For the rest of her shortened stay she slept with it clasped to her chest and the 'thing' never came back.

Now I have to say that listening to Mum tell us the story, we didn't believe her. We were all sympathetic, but I think we were all mentally measuring her for a jacket with no armholes. Poor Mum, she'd finally gone ga-ga.

However, things settled down at home and Mum didn't have any more 'episodes', and we all pretty much forgot about it.

About a year later I went across to stay with Sis. I sat on the train and gazed out the window, and the closer I got to the coast, the more Mum's experience played on my mind. I watched the misty hills and all that bush, I felt that anything was possible 'over here'.

Sis had made up the guest bedroom for me but I wimped out entirely. I chose to sleep in the junk room rather than use the back bedroom. Sis and her husband Gordon poked a bit of fun at me. They were convinced that Mum had just had nightmares those couple of nights.

By halfway through the second week of my stay nothing strange had happened and I was feeling a tad foolish. Though I must admit I did find this particular township a little strange. Gordon was at work most days, and Sis and I would take Debbie, who was a pre-schooler, out for walks around the town. It always felt kind of eerie.

I think some of the old towns on the coast have that effect. There is the constant mist and rain. The bush-clad hills crowd in, and there are lots of old derelict houses, remnants from the boom days of the gold, coal and timber industries.

Whatever, this little town really did send out some strange vibrations.

One night I was leaving the bathroom, which was at the kitchen end of the hall, having been built off the renovated kitchen to take advantage of the new wetback stove and all that lovely hot water.

There at the far end of the hallway, a distance of perhaps 20 feet away, was a big dog. It was trotting away from me down the hall. Then it took a left turn and went into the back bedroom.

Sis and Gordon didn't own a dog so I was puzzled. I ducked my head into the kitchen and asked Sis who owned the dog.

She looked at me as if I were mad. 'What dog?'

'The one that just went into the back bedroom,' I said. 'A big black dog.'

Sis immediately came out into the hallway and we went to the back bedroom. It was only then that I realised the door was closed, and I knew I hadn't closed it. In fact, from where I had been standing when I saw the dog, I couldn't tell whether the door had been open or not.

'Okay, so where's the dog?' asked Sis as she opened the door and we both looked inside. Of course there was no dog.

To Sis, it probably looked as if I had joined Mum in the loopy-loo stakes. But I knew damn well what I had seen. I had seen a big black short-haired dog in the hallway. It had been as real as any I had ever seen. That's why when I saw the animal I didn't yell. I guess subconsciously I assumed that visitors must have arrived and brought the dog with them, and it was just nosing around as dogs are wont to do.

Next day when we went walking I made a point of stopping to talk to an old man who lived a few doors down. Sis and I used to say hello every day as he sat on his verandah smoking his pipe and watching the world go by.

This particular day I struck up a conversation and asked him who had lived in Sis's house before the railways had bought it.

'Strange old foreign couple,' he said. 'They were here before I came, and that was 60 years ago. Didn't mix, didn't work. People said they had money. Never saw any sign of it. Once a week they would go down to the store. They never said more than they needed to. Bought what they wanted, paid cash and went back to the house. Curtains always pulled. Had two dogs.'

At the mention of dogs my ears were flapping, and Sis looked sideways at me.

'What sort of dogs?' I asked. The old-timer thought for a moment.

'Don't know the breed,' he said, 'just big, black mean-looking things. They didn't leave the property, but they would sit just inside the fence and watch everyone and everything that went past. The local kids were terrified of them. I wasn't too keen either, but they never attacked anyone. One thing,' he stopped to light his pipe and Sis and I waited, and waited.

Eventually, the old fellow got his smelly old pipe going. 'We didn't know until later, after the house was bought by another couple, that the dogs used to come and go into the place through a hole that the old people had cut in the floor of that bedroom at the back.'

Sis was suddenly looking a bit strange.

'What happened to the old people in the end?' I asked. I suppose I had a young girl's vision of murder, mayhem and deeds most foul. Pure Nancy Drew stuff.

The old man tossed that one right out the window. 'One day a truck came. They loaded most of their things on it and drove away but they left the dogs behind. They hung around for a while. The police constable at the time was talking of shooting them – they were pretty old by then. But no one could get near them. Some people threw bones over the fence to them. Then one day they were both gone. Must have gone bush and died I suppose.'

Sis and I thanked the old man and went on with our walk. Sis didn't say much but I think her mind must have been working overtime. I know that she and Gordon moved to another house a few weeks after I returned home to Christchurch.

She told me a few years later that after they moved out, some other railways people had moved in. Eventually Sis and Gordon heard on the grapevine that their old house had mysteriously burned down. It had been untenanted for quite some time. Apparently people just couldn't stay there, although no one could say why.

That was my one experience with the supernatural. I don't really want another. I can't help wondering though – do dogs have spirits?

The Power of Pounamu

In the early 1970s a friend (let's call him Andy) was hunting in the southwest of the South Island. There were a lot of guys working for venison recovery companies in the huge roughly rectangular area that stretched from Te Anau in the east across to Jacksons Bay, and north to Whataroa and through to Mount Cook. Helicopters, fixed-wing aircraft and jetboats were everywhere, carrying shooters and supplies in and venison out.

Some of the rivers in the south-west contain greenstone – New Zealand jade or pounamu. This hard stone was prized by the ancient Maori for making tools and implements. It was extremely valuable as a trade item and they travelled the length and breadth of the country to gather the precious stone. In more modern times pounamu has become prized for its ornamental value and it is protected by law in its natural sites.

It was while based at Jacksons Bay that Andy had the following experience. Note that the Waiatoto River is not the true location.

My pilot Les and I had come back to our base near Neil's Beach at Jacksons Bay at last light from a very successful sortie. We put down beside the company cooler that was the focus of our little temporary community. There were four old caravans, a tin shed for fuel and junk, a rickety long-drop and a few battered Land Rovers and utes littering the place. That was home away from home for three chopper crews and the odd hanger-on.

It took us five minutes to hang our catch in the cooler and then Les flew across to our caravan and parked the chopper for the night while I detoured to the long-drop. There was no sign of Morty's little Hughes 300. This wasn't unusual. Quite often we would get weathered in or simply run out of light and put down somewhere for the night. Most of us carried sleeping bags, a tent and basic supplies in the boot.

Les and I had cleaned up, opened a beer and started a meal when we heard the distinctive buzz of a 300.

'Morty coming in on a wing and prayer!' muttered Les, poking his head out the door. It wasn't quite pitch black but it was pretty dark. Morty's brother Alex, who looked after things on the ground for us, had his old Land Rover parked by the coolstore with the headlights on. As the chopper dropped into the light we could see there were a couple of animals hanging from the strop under the machine.

Les stood watching while I stirred the stew or whatever it was on the old spirit stove. Then it started to rain so Les came in and shut the door. Rain was the one thing we could depend on down in this part of the world.

It was after we'd eaten that the door crashed open and Morty and his shooter, Jed, came in.

'Come in, won't you?' said Les sarcastically as the pair of them stood dripping water all over the floor.

'Have a look at this, you guys.' Morty was carrying something in his arms. He dropped the object on the plywood table, just about breaking the table in half.

The piece of greenstone was about 18 inches long and six inches wide. It was rounded at one end and broken at the other. It was almost cylindrical in shape, with no sharp edges apart from the broken end.

I'd seen plenty of greenstone around. I think we all had a piece or two we'd picked up from the riverbed at some time or other. The difference was that this piece was polished. Normally it would have a dark, dull grey-green surface from weathering and the only bright bits would be where it had been broken off a larger bit or had a chunk freshly knocked out of it. In fact in its natural state it's hard to tell pounamu from ordinary rock without using a hammer to break the surface layer. I've actually had smoko sitting on a normal-looking river rock the size of a car, and it was only when I saw the colour in a crack in the boulder that I realised what it was.

This piece of greenstone of Morty's looked as if it had been carved from a boulder and had already been polished. There was no weathered surface at all. It wasn't a really deep green, it was quite light, with a kind of yellow tinge to it. It was very unusual.

'A beaut, isn't it?' Morty rolled the rock over so we could see the other side. It also was quite smooth and the same sort of amber green colour. 'Look at the colour – this is premium. Hardly any flaws.'

Les and I had to admit he was right. I'd never seen such an unusual colour and I'd certainly never seen a piece as polished outside of the factory in Hokitika.

'Where did you get it?' Les asked.

Morty just shook his head and laughed. 'We were chasing a deer up a creek. Jed shot it and when we parked up this was just lying there. I reckon there's more as well. We might just have to do a little prospecting.'

Morty looked well pleased with himself. Legally the greenstone had to stay put, but there was a big black market if you knew where to look. Some outfits had been poaching boulders of the stuff for years and there had been a couple of prosecutions and hefty fines. But it was hard to resist the temptation and a small perfect piece like this was worth more than a ton of poorer-quality jade.

'See you guys.' Morty picked up his prize and he and Jed puddled their way outside heading for their own caravan.

I didn't think anything more of that rather unusual piece of greenstone for a few days. The weather closed in and Les and I took the opportunity to drive up to Hokitika where Les lived with his wife Marie and their two kids. They had a sleepout in the back yard and it was here that I had made my home for the last year or so.

The weather was starting to look like clearing by day three and we were about to head south when a neighbour of Les's came over.

'Chopper down in the Waiatoto,' he said.

'Who?' Les and I asked together. 'Dunno. Just heard on the radio. No names.'

Les and I looked at each other. We didn't say a word but we knew damned well who it was. None of the meat machines would be in the air in this weather so it must have been someone on another mission.

'Better get going, eh?' Les said. Because we were running a turbine-powered 500 we had more grunt and better bad-weather flying capabilities than the older piston-engined choppers. If someone had to go in looking for the downed machine, it may well have to be us.

The drive back to Neil's Beach was a fast one. We stopped for a few minutes at Waiatoto and confirmed that it was Morty and Jed. A foot party had gone up the river, which was in half flood. If the chopper had landed on the riverbed it was probably gone. Morty had managed to radio out to his brother Alex that they were in big trouble but he had been cut off mid-sentence. Alex had raised the alarm.

When we got back to base all the guys were there. It was just about dark and still raining, but there were three or four choppers lined up ready to go at first light.

It was agreed next morning that because Les and I had the grunt machine we would scream off up the Arawata and climb up towards Aspiring before following the Waiatoto back down towards the sea. The others would sweep up from the sea. Some of the guys didn't have decent radios, which was a problem, but we figured we'd get around that somehow.

When they were finally spotted it was clear Morty and Jed had been very lucky. It turned out they had made a dry but hard landing after their chopper had had a fuel blockage. Fortunately they were high enough to auto-rotate down to an almost treeless plateau above the river. The chopper was severely damaged and the guys were well stirred and shaken, but otherwise okay.

They had been spotted by the ground searchers and by the time the airborne troops arrived they were ready to move out. Les and I took Morty and Jed out, the other machines queued up to give the searchers a welcome lift home. Later Morty's employers flew a mechanic in on a Jet Ranger so the damaged machine could be cleaned up and lifted out in a couple of pieces after the air accident inspector had done his thing.

Morty and Jed were back in the air a week later in another 300. A week after that, they crashed a second time, and this time they weren't so lucky: Jed suffered a broken back.

Les and I went north to do a clean-up job on goats in the Marlborough Sounds shortly after Morty's big crash. After that the company sent us to Australia to do some work on buffalo in the Northern Territories. It was two months before we arrived back in the south.

Morty was flying again, but I got a real shock when I first saw him. He'd always been a bit of a barrel – round face, big grin. Now he was almost skinny, his face was thin and he hardly smiled. He was nervous, chain-smoking and he was on the booze big time.

Shooters didn't like flying with him any more. He couldn't find animals, and when he did he couldn't get in position for the kill. The company was threatening to sack him if he didn't produce the goods and the stress was grinding him down. I found out from a mutual friend that his wife had left him. He'd also had a bad car crash when he was over in Christchurch. He'd been drunk and someone had been severely injured and there was big court case coming up.

We all tried to cheer Morty up but nothing worked.

In the air Les and I quickly got back in the groove and were taking good numbers. We'd watch Morty come in sometimes with nothing or with only one animal on the strop.

The axe eventually did fall and when it did, Morty had no chopper to fly. Fortunately, maybe, the whitebait season was starting in the south and he managed to get a job on one of the stands over on the Cascade. We didn't see much of him after that. Alex had another crew to look after and life went on.

There was a bad flood on the Cascade halfway through the season, which is not unusual in itself, but the outfit Morty was working for was the only one to get totally cleaned out. They decided not to rebuild their stand; the season hadn't been a good one anyway. So Morty was out of a job again. He flew back into Neil's Beach a couple of days later on a bait run.

Les and I went over to Alex's caravan to see Morty. I don't know to this day what drew my eye to it, but there beside the door was the piece of greenstone he'd shown us all those months ago.

'Still got your greenstone, eh?' I said.

'Yeah, it's my doorstop. I never got around to selling it. I guess I'd better now – I need the money,' he said.

I knew that the right person would pay a small fortune for that piece.

Morty stayed on at the beach to look after the chopper crew while Alex took a break. Les and I shot up to Hokitika for our own break a week or so later.

We were in the pub one night when the subject of pounamu came up. The latest poaching claim had gone through the court in Greymouth and the fine had a lot of zeros in it. There was talk of confiscation of vehicles and all sorts of other things as well.

One of our party that night was Isaac, a West Coast Maori. He was a true gentleman of the old school, aged somewhere between 70 and 90. Isaac wore a suit and tie everywhere, together with old-style leather zip-up slippers lined with sheepskin. He had arthritis in both hips and walked with the help of an elaborately carved walking stick with an ornate bone handle. It was a real work of art.

Isaac never said a lot. He arrived at the pub at precisely four o'clock every afternoon, dropped off by his daughter. She would pick him up again at six. Isaac would get his jug of beer and his glass – or rather Barry the publican would see him coming and carry them to the big leaner in the corner where we gathered. There was a stool there especially for Isaac. When he was there it was his. If any outsider was sitting on it when Isaac came in, he would get the message loud and clear from the publican or any local who was handy.

Once he was settled on his throne, Isaac would give us all a big smile. 'Hello boys. Nice to see you!' That would be about the extent of his conversation. Unless asked a direct question, Isaac would just sit and quietly drink his two jugs, seemingly content just to be among company.

This day was different. We'd talked about the greenstone poaching and the conversation moved on. It was me who mentioned the unusual piece I'd seen, but I didn't say where. Then I mentioned the hard luck that Morty was experiencing. I was only halfway through the catalogue of disasters when Isaac spoke.

'Tell him to put it back where he found it!' He was angry and his voice was surprisingly powerful. We all looked at him. He was standing beside his stool looking really upset. He was getting ready to leave and it wasn't even 4.30.

'Tell your friend to put the pounamu back where he found it and everything will be as it was.' Isaac started out of the pub and we all just stood looking after him. We'd never heard him raise his voice before – and he had gone when he hadn't even finished the first jug!

I was tempted to go after him but I had no idea why or what I would say to him. We were a little more subdued after that. Isaac didn't come into the pub the next day, and Les and I went down south again that evening.

The moment we arrived back at the beach we went to Alex's caravan. Morty had gone and Alex didn't know where. The greenstone doorstop was gone as well. Les and I told Alex what Isaac had said and that if Morty got back in touch, he should tell him.

It was maybe six months later when Les and I were working down on the Dart River, based at Glenorchy, when a new Hughes 500 landed beside us as we were shutting up shop for the day. We watched the pilot get out of the strange chopper and came across to us. It was Morty – the old Morty. He was at least three stone overweight and had a big grin.

It was hugs all round, then we adjourned to the pub for a beer.

'I want to thank you guys,' Morty said to us.

'For what?'

'That business with the greenstone. I was in Dunedin, had a buyer lined up – fancy jeweller, top price and all – and Alex caught up with me. Told me what you'd said. I thought about everything that had happened and I realised it had all started when I found that pounamu.

'So I took your advice. I hitched a ride back down south with one of the boys and flew in and put it back exactly where I found it. A week later I'm flying again. Breezed through my jet rating a month ago and got this ride. Janie and I are back together again better than ever. So thanks.' He raised his glass in a toast and we joined him.

We had a great night and neither Les nor I objected to Morty shouting. I just wish Isaac had been there. He deserved the thanks.

When we were next back in Hokitika and the pub, old Isaac was sitting in his seat sipping at his beer. I got a jug and went over to the corner.

'He put it back,' I told him.

He smiled. 'I know.'

We never mentioned it again.

The Spirit of the Ship

It's not surprising really that sailors are a superstitious lot. They sail the seas by grace of nature or God or both, depending on your persuasion. As a former seaman myself I can vouch for the fact that it is only when you face the wrath of the sea first hand that you realise just how fragile humans and their craft really are. That's when we cling to the concept of greater spirits and their ability to grant us salvation. This tale was told to me by a former shipmate.

The ship was the inter-island ferry *Maori*. She was a wonderful old vessel, a favourite of all who sailed and worked on her. The old girl was full of idiosyncrasies: deep brown wooden-panelled corridors, unexpectedly steep companionways, dark corners, passenger cabins that ranged from basic to luxurious and were priced accordingly.

Who will ever forget 'steerage', the dormitory accommodation right down in the bow, where every sea caused the bunks (and often the occupants) to heave? The new stewards always got the dormitories as their initiation to life at sea. After a big southerly on the overnight trip it was a great mess to clean up. That was 'Welcome to the *Maori*, lads!'

Crew accommodation was also basic in the extreme, with crowded cabins and small communal areas. It was a military lifestyle but we survived, and we had a lot of fun.

The *Maori* had been refitted and upgraded at various times in her life prior to her eventual role as a drive-on, drive-off vehicle and passenger ferry. There was something different about her as a vessel compared with those that followed. It wasn't just the way she was built or finished, with all that wood instead of plastic or steel. There was a real feeling about the ship, a spirit if you like. I don't think there was anyone who sailed the *Maori* regularly, passengers or crew, who failed to recognise that.

I remember a painting that hung prominently in one of the foyer landings. It was of a proud Maori chieftain in full moko, wearing a feather cloak. The painting was hanging there when I joined. I heard it had been presented and hung with all due ceremony when the ship was commissioned.

Whatever its origins, to most of us the name of our ship was synonymous with the existence of the painting . I don't think any of us dwelt on it.

But I guess looking back, the painting possibly gave a face to the spirit that we felt lived aboard with us.

There are many tales concerning the *Maori*; every crew member probably has one to tell. This is mine.

We were sailing south from Wellington to Lyttelton on a daylight sailing heading straight into a roaring southerly. To say it was uncomfortable would be a vast understatement. It was the pits.

When we had left Wellington it had been a steady blow but basically okay. The forecast had been for a southerly, but not gale-force winds. We were used to the southerly and the easterly, which were the prevailing winds on the route. But this one really cut up rough two or three hours into the trip.

We'd got across Cook Strait no problems, and were nearing Kaikoura, which is just under halfway, when all hell started to break loose. The trouble with that stretch of water is that there is nowhere to hide – in fact there was nothing but Banks Peninsula between us and the Antarctic, and we were a long, long way from the shelter of the peninsula.

As the 'tiger' or personal steward for the captain, I had the job of preparing trays of coffee and sandwiches in the officers' pantry and taking them up to the bridge as required. Normally I'd take one up as we were leaving port. The skipper would see the ship out of port, then retire to his cabin, letting the mate take over. The duty steward looked after the bridge from then on.

However, when faced with a potential 'situation' as on this day, the skipper stayed on the bridge and the tiger had to look after him and whoever else was up there. I hated days like this, because it meant I had to do my balancing act several times a day, instead of what was usually a cruisy trip.

And a balancing act it certainly was on this particular sailing. The companionway from the officers' accommodation deck to the bridge was steep at the best of times, particularly when you were carrying a tray loaded with hot liquids. More than once I reckon that as the ship rose and fell in the huge seas I floated at least halfway up the companionway without touching anything but the railing. Coming down on more than one occasion I resembled a circus performer who missed his trapeze. But I was lucky: I never sustained any serious injury.

On this trip and others where it was really bad, hot water, coffee and tea were all carried in flasks, and the milk and sugar in plastic containers. They were all tucked into a specially designed compartmentalised carry-bag.

I had the bag hooked over my shoulder. The mountain of sandwiches I had made were on the tray with dampened teatowels over the top to hold them down and keep them fresh. I got up to the bridge intact and, once there, I hung on with my toes and teeth and landed my cargo safely in the chart room.

Mission accomplished, I did what I always used to do, and that was have a nosy while I caught my breath. The *Maori* had an old-fashioned or traditional bridge. The wheel was a big wooden affair set in the central position. Radar console and compass and the like were all free-standing units.

Today the skipper, the first mate, third mate, bosun and helmsman were all on the bridge. It was pretty serious when they were all up there, I can tell you. From up there on the high point on the ship, the pitching and shuddering of the old girl was pretty rugged.

The man at the wheel, Den, was a big fellow about my age. He was working pretty hard following the instructions from skipper. Anyone who thinks that ships travel in a straight line as a matter of course is mistaken. There is no such thing as a straight line at sea. The movement of the water and the wind see to that.

The helmsman is continually making changes to the course. To help him on many vessels, the *Maori* included, there is a set of red and green lights representing port and starboard set above and in front of the wheel. Rather than call degrees from the compass, the officer would call, say, two green or three red or amidships (back to centre) to indicate which way to move the wheel. The helmsman would bring up his two green or three red lights, then, when called, let the wheel spin back to a position where the lights were all out (amidships).

Sounds simple, but when you are pounding into a southerly that has everyone on the ship hanging on for grim death it really isn't a simple matter to keep it pointing where you want it.

We were not far from Kaikoura when I overheard the skipper tell the mate that if the opportunity arose, he wanted us to turn back to Wellington. The forecast was predicting worse weather to come. I handed out my coffee and sandwiches. The bosun, Ossie, relieved Den on the wheel and I gave him a mug of coffee and a ham sandwich. We talked for as long as it took for him to get through his coffee and two sandwiches.

'Bloody tough hanging on to the old girl,' he said to me at one stage.

'She really wants to go back to Wellington.'

The way the seas were coming at us I didn't think there was any chance of a break that would allow the ship to be turned safely. I'd had a few stints on the wheel and I knew just how slowly a ship that size responded. We would have needed possibly two minutes in flat water to turn back on our course and there weren't two minutes here without a 20- or 30-foot swell coming in. We were just bashing into the big seas one after another.

It wasn't just the swells that were the problem either. In fact if anything the swells were probably being clipped and held down slightly by the wind. Turning across the water direction would be bad enough, but add to that a gale that was going to use the superstructure of the ship as a sail, and we would not be able to turn back without capsizing.

No way. Lyttelton here we come, I thought to myself.

Den went back on the wheel and I gave the bosun his coffee and sandwiches. The skipper suggested that I 'keep the provisions coming'. With that, I headed down the companionway with my tray and my carrier of empty flasks.

It's a funny thing about life on board ship but when you're busy you never think about sea sickness. Normally, in those sorts of conditions I and any other members of the crew who weren't working would have simply gone to our bunks and slept. Almost without exception, every sailor I've met reckons he could sleep anywhere at any time and I believe it.

I figured I had half an hour before I needed to start back on the sandwiches and brews, so I took the opportunity to head down to the crew quarters in the stern for a break. On the way I went down to the main passenger level to see how they were coping.

Because this was a summer daylight sailing, the ship was full of holiday-makers heading south. Poor things. There was vomit everywhere and shiny white faces (even the Maori passengers had shiny white faces that day). Stewards were rushing around with mops and buckets but it was a losing battle. In our quarters, off-duty stewards were drinking in the common room. The beer we all reckoned gave your stomach something to throw up and helped prevent dehydration. As a theory it mightn't hold water (as it were) but it worked for us.

I was making my way back through the upper corridor, which was closed off to passengers during the day, because I couldn't face looking at the sheer misery down on the main deck. I had just reached a point where a short side corridor cut across the main one. From this corridor doors opened out onto the deck on both sides. The doors each had a port-hole in them.

Suddenly the whole ship heeled right over to starboard. And boy, do I mean right over. For a long time I was standing with one foot on the deck and one on the corner of the bulkhead – basically I was caught between sliding off the floor and spread-eagling myself on the wall, or flying down the short corridor to my right and slamming into the door. I was alone in the corridor but I could hear people yelling, some screaming. There was the sound of breaking glass and crockery. The old girl was creaking and groaning, every part of her.

This is it! I was thinking. We had to go over – there was no way she could pull herself back up from this angle. Looking down beyond my right boot, I could see deep green/blue water through the port-hole in the door. It looked so close. We sort of hovered there in limbo for maybe a minute, although it seemed like a lifetime. Then we slowly, so slowly, came back onto an even keel.

The sea dropped away from the door. My feet were both back on deck.

I sprinted for the companionway and the door to get me up to the officers' level. When I opened the door into the officers' lounge first thing I saw was that the land wasn't where it should have been, away to my right. There was just open sea out there. I looked the other way, and there were the Kaikouras. We were heading back to Wellington. Now we were running with the seas, the old girl was wagging her tail and half surfing, but it was a damn sight better than smashing into that big southerly swell.

As part of the crash crew I headed for the bridge to see if I was needed.

I was halfway up the bridge companionway when I was met by Den, the helmsman, coming down. Adrian, the mate, who was medical officer, was supporting him. Den's right arm was in a sling on his left shoulder.

'I'll hand him over to you, Pat. Make him comfortable. Broken collarbone I think.'

The mate headed back up top and I took Den straight into the skipper's cabin because it was nearest. I got him parked on a couch and poured him one of the old man's scotches, a big one. Medicinal of course. I had one myself.

'What happened?' I asked. Den took a good slug of whisky before he spoke.

'The old girl decided she wanted to go back to Wellington, simple as that, Pat. I was hanging on keeping the course and next thing you know, she just decided to turn. I was thrown halfway across the bridge. I hit the radar console full on, then the deck. Man, did it hurt.

'Adrian and Ossie got the wheel but they couldn't move it, neither of them. She just keep coming round. They couldn't get an inch back off her. Then when she was right around, the wheel just turned to butter. Ossie was holding her with one finger when I left.'

Eighteen stone or so of Den had simply been tossed aside when the *Maori* decided she wanted to go home. Two other able-bodied men on the wheel couldn't budge her until she had completed her turn. In real life things like that don't happen – or do they?

Strangely enough, although there was quite a lot of superficial damage inside the ship there was nothing really serious. Crockery and glassware went down in heaps, and quite a few passengers and crew needed patching up, but Den was the most seriously injured with a broken collarbone and a few broken ribs. Some vehicles and cargo were also damaged but not too badly.

That night, once we were tied up and cleaned up, a few beers were drunk over at the Waterloo Hotel. We all discussed what had happened and all agreed that the old girl had decided enough was enough and taken matters into her own hands, turning us back.

How she didn't roll right over no one knew. Every ship has a gauge on the bridge that shows degrees of roll and the *Maori* that day sent the needle right off the clock. Yet somehow she came back up.

All the official checks were made of course. There was no steering fault, no rudder damage. The old girl had simply decided to turn back. Den was back on the wheel a month or so later. It had never happened to him before and never happened again.

If I didn't believe in the spirit of that ship before that day, I sure as hell did from then on.

I always enjoyed the *Maori* and all her quirks. A while later she was decommissioned and was still in Wellington Harbour before being sailed away for the last time. We would sail past her every day and I couldn't help feeling a nostalgic twinge.

Her replacement, the *Rangatira*, had serious mechanical problems at one stage early in her career and went off to Hong Kong or somewhere for repairs. To fill the gap, the company fired up the old *Maori* and put her back on the Lyttelton-Wellington route.

For a lot of the crew it was like a sort of homecoming. Yes, aboard the *Rangatira* the accommodation was far better; we had two-man or single cabins. Yes, the new ship was easier to clean and maintain; yes, it was more comfortable and had better facilities for passengers and crew. But there was something missing.

Those last few weeks on the Maori before it was all over for her were great days. I know I wasn't the only one that missed her when she finally went. The others ships I worked on over the years just never had that spirit.

The Woman in the Chair

The events in this story took place shortly after World War II.

Two of my brothers and I went away to war at the same time. We were all off to fight Rommel in the desert. In a way, it was our big adventure. We didn't think about dying – I suppose we were all too young and stupid.

War to us was an abstract and the three of us couldn't wait to join up, much to Mum's despair. Her father had been gassed in the first war and took five long years to die. I was too young to know him or the lessons watching his death might have taught me.

It must have been hell for Mum and Dad watching us sail away. Their 'boys' – all three of us gone together. There were no more left at home and there never would be any more. Much as Mum loved Megan and Ann, our two sisters, I think her boys had a special place in her heart.

Anyway, David and I ended up prisoners of the Italians, while Ian was killed in Crete. Undoubtedly the news of Ian's death and the lack of news about her other two sons contributed to the heart condition that took Mum's life in late 1944. She died not knowing whether David and I were alive or not.

We were eventually liberated and when Germany surrendered, our outfit was sent home. We arrived home on 8 August 1945, two days after the bombing of Hiroshima, one day before Nagasaki. The war was over for us.

We were demobbed and David and I walked out of Trentham as civilians. Dad and the girls were waiting for us. They were still living in the family home at Kilbirnie, Wellington, and Dad had somehow scrounged enough petrol to fill his old Chevrolet.

The homecoming was an emotional time. The neighbours all came over and there was a big party, but under it all there was a great sadness. Mum had gone, and so had Ian.

David and I had done a lot of growing up in a very short time. I was 22, David was 24. I think we both felt like much older and wiser men. I think also that the two of us blamed ourselves and our eagerness to join up for Mum's death.

That first afternoon we ate, drank and put on merry faces, more for Dad and the girls and everyone else than for ourselves. We had perhaps grieved for Ian, but we hadn't had an opportunity to grieve for Mum.

THE WOMAN IN THE CHAIR

When the house eventually quietened down I went up to my old room. The girls had it sparkling clean. There were fresh flowers and the mattress seemed so soft. I lay down for a few minutes and must have gone straight to sleep.

I woke up at some stage during the night. Someone had taken my shoes off and pulled a rug over me. I needed to go to the bathroom so I got out of bed and quietly went downstairs.

The bathroom was at the back of the house. There was a toilet upstairs, but it always woke the whole house so I didn't use it at night.

I was tiptoeing past the lounge when for some reason I looked in. There were no lights on, just the glow from the dying fire, which had a screen in front of it.

It's amazing what you can take in at a glance. I was past the door when I realised that there had been someone, a woman, sitting in the chair to the left of the fire. I saw her shape plainly. She had knitting needles in her hands, and a ball of wool was sitting on the mat in front of the fire screen.

I thought it must have been one of the girls. I carried on out to the toilet, and when I came back I stuck my head around the lounge door to say hello. There was no one there. Whichever one it had been had obviously decided it was time for bed.

The hall clock struck one as I made my way back up to my room. I didn't seem to think it at all strange that one of my sisters might have been sitting in an almost totally darkened room knitting.

Breakfast was a real family affair. Despite rationing, Dad and the girls had got hold of bacon and eggs. There was butter, marmalade and beautiful thick toast. It definitely was the best breakfast that David and I had had in three or so years.

'Who was knitting in the lounge last night?' I asked at one point.

Dad looked at the girls, then at David and me. Megan and Ann were both shaking their heads. Then Ann in particular started looking a little upset.

'What time?' asked Dad.

'I came down to the toilet at about one,' I said.

Ann stood up and rushed from the kitchen. Megan excused herself and followed her out.

Dad lit a cigarette and offered the pack to David and me. We were both smokers then. We all lit up and Dad told us what had happened to Mum.

Dad was a member of the local volunteer watch group. The night Mum died he had been on duty. The girls were at home with Mum, who had been feeling okay for a few days. They had dinner, then Megan had gone across the road to see a college friend. Ann had gone to her room to study, leaving Mum sitting knitting in her chair in front of the fire.

Megan came home at about 10 o'clock, made Mum and herself a cup of tea and a cocoa for Ann. They all sat in front of the fire until they had finished, when the girls offered to help Mum to bed. She replied that she was fine and that she would just sit and knit until Dad got in. He was normally back by midnight.

The girls stoked the fire, put the screen in front of it, kissed Mum goodnight and went to their rooms. Megan's was upstairs, Ann's was downstairs at the back of the house.

But that night Dad was held up. There was an accident at the railyards and the watch crew volunteers were all sent to help clear things up.

Ann had to go to the bathroom during the night and noticed that the table lamp was still on in the lounge. Thinking Mum and Dad had forgotten to turn it off, poor kid, she walked in and found Mum dead in her chair by the fire.

It must have been a very peaceful death. Mum still had her knitting on her knee – the needles were still in her hands. Ann at first thought she was just asleep but when she saw that Mum wasn't breathing she rushed screaming from the room to get Megan.

Dad arrived home to find the doctor there. Mum's death was put down to heart failure and the time of death was estimated at one o'clock.

Poor little Ann. She was only 13 and the shock of discovering Mum really did disturb her. She blamed herself and had nightmares for years afterwards.

Well, Dad finished the story, and suggested that perhaps I had been dreaming the night before. I didn't argue, but I thought it uncanny that all the details matched the night of Mum's death.

That night I again went downstairs late but there was no figure sitting in the chair in the lounge. I started to think that maybe Dad was right and it was a dream. That was until David took me aside the next morning as we were going to breakfast. He was upset.

'I saw her, Paul. Last night. I came down to the loo and I looked in and she was there. I went in. Mum just turned her head and smiled at me, then she wasn't there any more.'

David was almost crying.

We never did see Mum's 'ghost' again. I'm not into spirits and things as such. What I do know though is that a figure that I believe was my mother's spirit was sitting there when I walked past the lounge that night. I believe David when he says that he saw her as well.

Perhaps because her boys were away on the other side of the world when she died and Mum didn't know if we were alive or dead, her spirit – ghost, essence, call it what you like – waited for our return.

It was unfinished business. She wanted to see her boys. When we came home she was waiting. Once she had seen both of us she was happy and she moved on.

Over the next 20 years that the house remained in our family we never had another 'spiritual' experience. I have never seen another ghost, and I doubt that I ever will.

The Sand Dog

This tale, like some others, has been told to me (with minor variations) by several people. In this story the location has always been the same. This particular version is from a person who has seen the apparition a number of times.

I live in a seaside settlement. It is a pleasant little place just north of a major river mouth. It's a place filled with retired people and holiday homes – a nice little community. We fish for salmon, sea-run trout, whitebait and ocean fish throughout the year, and because we have miles of uninterrupted beach stretching away to the north, we walk the sands a lot. In fact, for many of us, those long walks in the bracing sea breeze filled with the salt tang of the Pacific are one of life's greatest pleasures.

As you can imagine, many of us have dogs for companionship. Beaches, retired folk and dogs go together: it's one of nature's perfect little equations.

The first time I encountered the Sand Dog was 10 years ago but it has been on the beach for much longer than that. Some of the really old people in the village say that their parents used to talk about it. If that is true, it means that the Sand Dog has been in existence for the better part of a hundred years.

I'd always watched for it when I was walking my dog, or just wandering by myself along the beach or the sand dunes that border it.

The Sand Dog is a big dog – a black dog. No one knows what breed it is. All they know is that it is big and black, and it is seen at certain times on the beach. Those times will become clear as you read this.

The reason it is called the Sand Dog is quite simply because it is only ever seen down on the sand. Some of the old people call it the Black Dog but there are many flesh-and-blood black dogs that visit the beach and only one Sand Dog.

On this particular day I was by myself. My wife had died a few months previously and I spent a lot of time simply walking with my thoughts. There is something deeply spiritual about the sea.

Now our old dog had died a few months before Emily, and so far I had not succumbed to the pressure being exerted on me by my family and friends to get myself another pet. The time wasn't right for me.

THE SAND DOG

I was walking along the hard sand down near the water's edge and was about two miles north of the river mouth. It was a pretty unpleasant day. There had been rain, there was no sun and a cold wind was blowing, but I was wearing a thick coat and at the time didn't really notice the weather. What I did notice was the fact that I was the only person on the beach. I reached the point where I normally turn back for home. This was where a huge tree stump had washed ashore in a storm many years before. It had been washed right to the spring tide line and had sat there all those years, a giant gnarled mass of wood half the size of a three-room bach.

I turned and started slowly for home, and it was then that I saw the black figure through the salt spray. It was a long way off and close to the water's edge. My eyesight wasn't great even then, but it wasn't too bad. I saw the shape as big and dog-like. I didn't think of the Sand Dog. It was just a dog and I figured its owner was probably further down towards the river. It's not unusual for the local dogs to go off and run themselves. The beach is a natural playground for everyone and everything.

I trudged on and the black dog kept coming towards me. Now, those of you who walk beaches will know how deceptive distances can be. Things either look miles away or, under certain light and visibility conditions, much closer than you'd expect. The black dog still seemed to be a long way away. It was bounding towards me but seemed not to be getting any closer.

I just kept walking and I suppose I subconsciously focused on it. Suddenly the dog seemed much bigger, much closer. It was running very intently towards me on a collision course – one of us would have to step aside. I was walking on the line of hard sand above the wave line, and that was where the dog was running.

I wasn't at all concerned. I get on well with animals, dogs in particular. I suppose the dog and I were maybe 200 yards apart now, and I was watching it to see what it would do. I was curious and, as it was the only thing on the beach apart from me, this dog had my undivided attention as I walked along.

I was looking straight at it when the animal vanished. One moment it was there; the next it wasn't. There was no flash of light, no sound, no sudden anything: it was there, then it wasn't. There was no cover for a hundred yards up to the sand dunes, just bare beach. It didn't run into the surf or turn into a seal: it was a dog, then it was nothing.

I kept my presence of mind. I've just seen the Sand Dog, I said to myself, quite calm. I kept walking, and when I got to where I figured the dog had been, I looked for doggy prints in the sand. There were none. Even though the sand was hard I left boot prints, and I knew from experience that a big dog's paws – particularly its nails, leave their imprint on anything short of rock.

I got home and made a cup of tea, and it was probably half an hour later that a neighbour called in with bad news. One of the local identities, an old lady known and loved by all in the community, had just died.

'You were out walking when it happened,' my friend told me. I didn't mention seeing the Sand Dog; it didn't seem appropriate at the time.

Later I did tell some of the others. That's the thing. Local legend has it that when the Sand Dog runs along the beach, it means someone is dying. Call it a silly superstition, call it anything you like, but I know what I saw that day and I know what happened.

Since that time I have seen the Sand Dog twice more, each time several years apart, and each time someone in our community has died. Others have seen it as well, and it appears that is the way it goes.

Perhaps one day soon someone will see it and it will be my time.

No Photographs, Please

This tale was told to me by Josie, who is a member of a prominent North Island tribe. In 1997 Josie's family held a reunion on the tribe's traditional lands. Josie and several of her family members who live in Christchurch made the trip north and joined other family members in the week-long celebration. This is her story.

It was the biggest gathering of my whanau for many years – certainly the biggest in my lifetime. Family came from all over to be there, even from Australia.

It was a wonderful occasion. It was a chance for many of us younger ones to meet relatives we had never met before. I knew that I might never see many of the old people again and I relished the opportunity. There were so many wonderful people gathered in the one place at the one time – we numbered almost 100.

As part of the celebration we did a tour of several of the famous old pa sites. These were places I remembered from my childhood and from stories told to me by my grandmother. We also visited several marae, many of which were very special to our people and our family in particular.

One marae, where tapu had never been lifted, was regarded as possibly the most sacred place in our tribal land. Part of the reason for this was the nearby burial grounds. There were two of them. One is still used and many of our family are buried there, while the other burial ground goes back centuries. This older one is regarded as most sacred and admission is forbidden unless various formalities are observed. Then, a tohunga may escort people into the cemetery to pay their respects.

A great-grandfather of mine, a respected tohunga, is buried there, and the family wished to pay their respects so it was arranged that we could enter the burial ground.

We were instructed on the protocol. For many of us younger ones it was the first time we had ever been involved in this and it was a very serious business. We were instructed where we could walk, and told to be very careful not to stand on the graves.

We entered the burial ground with a tohunga and kaumatua leading us, and duly paid our respects. It was an emotional experience and one that I will treasure forever. The atmosphere at the marae and in the burial grounds was something special. There was a huge, warm feeling in the air – a very deep spirituality that touched us all. I have never experienced anything quite like it before and that is another thing that I will treasure about this gathering of our family. I cut off a lock of my hair and tied it in a tree so I would have a physical presence there for all time. To some people this may sound silly but to me it made sense.

There were about 40 of us who went to the marae and I guess about 10 or so, including myself, were carrying cameras. Over the week hundreds of rolls of film had been taken, including many shots at this special place. Of course we were not allowed to take photographs in the old burial ground, but I took a lot outside it, of people and the marae itself. Some of the others took only one or two shots and some, like me, took heaps.

At the end of this wonderful day I returned to the marae where we were staying and really did feel that it was a part of my heritage. I felt that the spirits of those who had gone before had really reached out to me on that magic day. The others felt it as well.

At the end of the week we said our tearful farewells and reluctantly left for our homes around the country. I'm sure that all of us felt gratitude for the fact that we knew where we had come from as a family and as a people. To me, it felt great. I had a focus that included the places and the faces of my family.

Back in Christchurch I had photographs developed – a very expensive and exciting exercise. I had gone crazy with my camera and taken literally hundreds of shots. Most were of family but there were a lot of the special places as well. I opened packet after packet of photos and spread the snaps all over the kitchen table. 'There's so and so. There's ... There's ...' It was like Christmas.

The last packet was of our special marae with the two burial sites. When I opened the packet I was amazed and at first upset. Of the 24 frames I had shot, only two had come out and these were of people I had photographed before and after we had been there. There was a sticker from the process company saying that there had been a fault with the film or camera, but there was nothing on the missing frames.

A few days later I mentioned to one of my relatives that the photographs I had taken at the marae hadn't come out. She stunned me when she said the three or four photos she had taken there also hadn't been printed.

I phoned another of my family who I knew had taken photographs there. The same thing. That did it. I rang around and spoke to everyone I could remember who had had a camera there that day. It was the same for everybody. Of all the photographs taken over that week, the only ones that hadn't come out were the ones taken at that particular marae.

I haven't tried to explain it — I can't. I only know that this was the way it was. Perhaps it was the tapu, perhaps the spirits of our ancestors were reaching out to us to tell us something. Whatever the reason, I can accept that it happened, and that this is just another magical thing about my visit to my ancestral home.

Taniwha Tarn

Donald Burn has worked for acclimatisation societies ever since he left school. He was in his early thirties when this incident occurred and had (he thought) seen everything that swam, flew or walked this country. A keen recreational hunter, Donald had ventured into the most remote parts of Fiordland into hidden corners that few have ever visited. He found no ghosts there.

However, one fine day Donald encountered something he has never been able to explain. Something that has given him new eyes as he goes about his job and his life in the great New Zealand outdoors.

It was early autumn and my offsider and I were doing a fish count in the many small lakes or tarns that litter a certain district in the South Island. Some of these tarns are not much bigger than ponds and many, in fact most, hold trout. A couple of them are home to the largest brown trout I have ever seen in over 30 years as a field officer.

The counting technique was very basic. On the smaller tarns Trevor and I would string a deep, fine-mesh flounder net across one end of the tarn, grab a rope each and draw the net down to the other end. There, we would gather the net in so it covered only a few square feet of water and count the fish. Baring a snag in the pond, the whole operation was simplicity itself. If we snagged, then one of us went for a wade or a swim to clear it.

On larger tarns the technique was different by necessity and it was 'get wet' time. Generally, only one of us suited up and went in with a snorkel. Depending on the size of the water area, and the weather and water conditions, the non-swimmer would be in our little dinghy as a safety measure. The swimmer would quarter backwards and forwards across the tarn taking a count. Strangely enough, the fish were not really disturbed by the movement of the diver so the counts were fairly reliable.

On our second day the weather was fine, with no wind and plenty of sun, so visibility in the water was reasonably good. We were starting on our second survey of the day. The two tarns we had scheduled were only half a mile apart, both sat on an area of tussock and grass with no trees for miles – no cover over 18 inches tall. These conditions incidentally made it very difficult to shoot this area during the duck season.

I had drawn the short straw on this day and Trevor was in the dinghy.

The tarn was almost circular and probably 200 yards across. It was a big swim that would take me a couple of hours. I was thankful for the extra-thick wetsuit but I knew I would still be cold by the time I finished. Trevor had a thermos of coffee in the boat so I could at least have a warm drink as we worked.

The first thing I noticed when I put my head under was nothing! Normally there were cockabullies and small trout everywhere in the shallows, but not so here. I noted it as unusual and started on my first beat. Normally in a populated tarn there would be trout every few feet within your line of vision. Some tarns had a population of up to 300 mature fish. We didn't count the fry.

The last time we had counted this particular pond, some two years previously, there had been 133 mature brown trout in it. Some of the fish had been in the 10-12-pound range, with most 2-4 pounds.

Today there was nothing. No fry, no trout whatsoever. I had been in the water for maybe 20 minutes and seen no sign of life, not even an eel. The tarns *always* had eels in them.

I wouldn't say I was getting uneasy, but I was wondering what on earth had happened here. If hoons had come in and stripped the waters of fish they wouldn't have taken the fry – they would have needed a whitebait mesh to get them out. Any chemical release, explosion or whatever would have left dead fish littering the mud on the bottom.

I stopped for a drink and a chat with Trevor, hanging off the end of the dinghy in about 10 feet of water.

'Nothing here!' I said as he handed me a mug of coffee. 'I haven't seen a fish the whole time!' Trevor was not surprised. Normally the one sitting around in the boat also sees quite a lot of fish movement and he'd seen nothing.

'What was that? Trevor was suddenly pointing down the tarn to where the water was moving. Something had dived.

'Probably a shag,' I replied.

'Too big for a shag,' said Trevor. 'Black. I just caught a glimpse.'

'I'll see it if it's down there because there's nothing else in here!' I handed Trevor back the mug, fitted my mask and snorkel and set off again.

Five minutes, 10 minutes and still nothing. It's a fact that small ponds with no big fish in them can be cleaned out by shags. But while the birds are gluttons, capable of swallowing quite large herring-size trout in a gulp, the big fish have nothing to fear from them. In fact I once saw a shag drowned by a big trout that grabbed its leg and pulled it under. Some might suggest that the trout was protecting its young but I think not. Big trout can be aggressive hunters and they'll eat anything, including their own young. The shag in question just got very unlucky.

As I swam I kept my eyes open for the shag or whatever bird had taken the plunge during my coffee stop. I had no doubt that whatever had made the splash was a bird. It never once entered my mind that it was a fish of any sort.

It was the banging that pulled my head up out of the water. Trevor was smacking the butt of his oar on the bottom of the boat.

'Don!' He was 20 feet away, shouting and pointing down the tarn. 'There's something in the water and its coming your way. It's bloody big! You wanna get in the boat?'

Even through the rubber of the head gear I could hear something approaching panic in his voice.

Trevor and I had worked together for about four years. We had pulled a lot of practical jokes on each other over those years, but I could tell he wasn't joking this time. I put my head back under, looking in the direction he had pointed, but I couldn't see anything. The water was clear for maybe 10 feet in any direction then sediment clouded it. I could hear the sound of Trevor rowing towards me.

What was going on? Then I saw a black shape through the murk. It sure was big. It was moving across my line of vision rather than straight at me. I couldn't see it clearly but it was several feet long, maybe the size of a very big dog, but it was swimming like a fish – there didn't seem to be any legs moving. Then it was gone, faded back into the cloudy water.

By now the boat was right on me. Trevor turned it and I grabbed hold of the stern and just about capsized us as I hauled myself in, scraping my shins, banging my head. I sat up and Trevor just about beaned me with the handle of an oar as he threshed the water.

'Slow down!' I said. 'Let's see what it is.' I managed to sit down and pull my head gear off. 'God it was big – look, there it is!'

We both saw it then. It was about 30 feet away, a black shape just below the surface of the water. It was moving very fast, parallel to us. Then it turned and came straight at us, diving deeper as it did so.

Trevor was flailing at the water again to get us moving while I was yelling at him to stop.

'We've got to see it! Stop!'

I was leaning down, watching the water. Whatever it was I wanted to put a name to it. Trevor had stopped rowing and then I saw it down near the bottom 10 or 12 feet below, moving very quickly right under us. It was black, about four or five feet long, pointed nose, body the size of my labrador. It had a long tail. It was gone under the boat in seconds.

Trevor and I made it to shore, both shaken. We stood without saying a word, watching the surface of the tarn. Nothing. The wind came up and the water got choppy but we didn't see a thing. Whatever it was hadn't come up to breathe that we could see, and there was no way a creature that size could have got out of the water unseen. There was coarse grass all around the tarn and cropped tussock from grazing sheep and cattle. We would have spotted a rabbit on the other side, let alone something of that size.

As part of my job I read a lot. I'd read the legend of the native otter years before. It was supposedly a giant member of the otter family that had lived here long before the European came, perhaps even before the Maori arrived.

Every now and then people still say they have seen an otter-like creature. Always the sightings have been fleeting and there are never any other physical signs – no dead animals, no droppings, no footprints, no sign of the creature feeding.

But something had taken the fish from that tarn. That was a fact. And Trevor and I had seen something we had never seen before. Had it been a creature that was extinct, if it ever lived here in the first place, or had we seen something else?

The question has never been answered. Trevor and I packed up our gear with an eye on the water, then we walked right around the tarn, looking for any signs that would help us to put a name to what we had seen. There were no animal or bird droppings that we couldn't identify and likewise no prints that didn't have a name. There were no remains of dead fish on the banks, no signs of anything we didn't know existed. As professional fish and game managers we recorded the event but no one had any answers. Some put it down to imagination. It wasn't.

From that moment on, whenever I dived to do a fish count I was always looking for that big shadow in the water. In almost 15 years since that day I have never seen it again.

The fish came back to the tarn when we restocked it a year later. There are still trout there today, untouched except by shags and anglers. Whatever had paid a visit to that tarn on that particular day has moved, maybe back into legend. I never give up hope of one day seeing it again and being able to put a name to it. Otter? Taniwha?

The Unhappy Tiki

The woman who told me this story was 93. She had enjoyed a long life of almost continuous good health and, some would say, good luck. I guess she led a charmed existence. She died peacefully in her sleep at 95, leaving behind two daughters, a son and countless grandchildren.

I was five, in my first year of school, at the time this story started. My family, which consisted of mother and father, my brothers Teddy and Derek, who were nine and seven respectively, and my older sister Kate who was 13, all went to the beach to picnic.

We lived in a small country town 10 miles from the sea. Father was a shopkeeper and because the shop was closed at weekends we often went visiting or exploring with a picnic.

Those were the days when not many people had cars. Father had a carriage that was pulled by two horses. He actually never owned a car in his entire life and he died in 1924. For our day at the beach the whole family climbed aboard father's wagon and we were away at a steady clip-clop.

It was on this particular day that something happened that I believe changed my life forever, although it would be several years before I realised it.

The beach where we went was surrounded by high sand dunes – what a marvellous place to play. We would play hide and seek and slide down the sand hills. There would be paddling and the older ones would swim.

I was making sandcastles with my bucket and spade where the sand was wet. The sand on this beach was fine and very white – that was what made it stand out. Suddenly I saw a little twinkle of green. When I lifted it from the sand and brushed it, what I saw made me jump up and run to show Father.

It was a tiki carved from greenstone. It was tiny – just an inch long and half an inch wide. There was a little hole in the head where it had been attached to something. Mother and Father said I could keep it.

For the rest of the day I had my little tiki in my hand. I would not let go of it. I would show my brothers and my sister but not let them touch it in case they grabbed it and ran away and lost it.

That night when we went got home Mother came to me with a little silver chain she had in her jewellery box. It was very fine and she threaded

THE UNHAPPY TIKI

it through the hole in the tiki and hung it around my neck. I was so proud. I couldn't wait to go to school and show my friends.

The next morning, Monday, I woke up feeling sick. Tummy bug was Mother's diagnosis. 'Too many sweets,' she said. Because of the shop we always had sweets. The boys and Kate used to steal them and we would eat them late at night, hiding under our bedclothes.

But the next day I was much worse. It seemed I had full-blown appendicitis and I was rushed to hospital, one very sick little girl. Appendicitis was very serious back then. It was about two weeks before I went home.

A week or so after that I was back in hospital again – this time with a broken leg. I had been climbing trees with a friend. A branch had broken and I had fallen.

Back home with my leg in plaster, I was hobbling around on some small crutches my father had made when I was bitten by our dog. I had accidentally put my crutch down on his tail and he snapped at me.

Calamity Jane became my nickname. At school I always seemed to be falling over. I never came home without extra bruises. I think Father and Mother were starting to worry that something very serious was wrong with me. All through the spring I was out of sorts with some complaint or other.

At Christmas we all took the train to go south and visit my uncle, Father's brother, and his family. They lived right by the sea – it was a lovely spot. One day when all of us children were swimming, an old Maori man who always sat on the rocks at the end of the beach fishing came over to where my cousins and I were making sandcastles.

He said to me, 'You shouldn't have that tiki on a chain. You will make it unhappy. You must put it on a string or on leather, then it will be happy and be lucky for you.'

With that, he walked away with his big bamboo fishing rod over his shoulder and his sugarbag of fish in his hand. My cousin Elizabeth, who was older than me by two or three years, asked if she could have the chain.

'Only if you get me something else to hang my tiki on,' I said. Elizabeth went away and I took my chain off. I didn't want an unhappy tiki. She came back with a leather bootlace that I found out later she had stolen from her father's best boots.

I gave Elizabeth the silver chain (which later on her mother made her give back to my mother). I threaded the little tiki on to the bootlace and Elizabeth tied a knot. When I put the tiki on, it felt 'right' in some way. Whether it was my childish imagination or not, it really did seem to be different.

My luck changed almost from that moment. Uncle John let me keep the bootlace. Father said he would send him down a new packet when we got home!

The old Maori man gave me a big smile when he saw me with the tiki on the leather next day. He touched it and held it in his hand for a moment. 'I think it belonged to a little girl like you once. It is happy. You will be lucky.'

We went home shortly after that and I never saw that man again. But I did stop bumping into things. I didn't seem to get sick any more. I always told people that my little tiki was lucky, and I believe it is. I met my husband David purely by luck. We married and had three wonderful, healthy children. He survived the Great War. We always had enough to eat and a nice place to live in. The children have all married and have given me many grandchildren. When David died peacefully in his sleep one night, we had been married 51 years. I expect that when my time comes, it will be the same for me.

When I do die, my little greenstone tiki will go to my youngest granddaughter. I hope it will bring her the luck that it has brought me, ever since I made it happy.

The Lady of the Lake

The man who told this story worked on many of the hydro-electric projects that were carried out in the 1950s and 60s in both the North and South Islands. He never believed in ghosts – except for one.

We were going through the latter stages of one of the big dam projects. Most of major work was done and the dam was slowly being filled.

I was driving a big dozer and as the waters slowly came up, about half a dozen other machine operators and I were working around what would be the eventual high-water mark.

Our job was to scrape boat ramps, haul away trees and generally tidy up the area. Some of the earlier dam efforts had left trees sticking out of the water and stuff like that. We were told none of that was to happen on this project, so apart from rocks, if it was going to be above low-water level, it was gone.

The area we were working on was really big. We had one team going up each side of the lake to be, with two dozers and a scraper in each team. The plan was to meet up at the top end, where there was going to be some major landscape work. Lots of boat ramps, some ponds and camping areas, tree planting, that sort of thing.

The water was actually coming in a bit more quickly than anyone had anticipated, but it was decided that rather than let water go in order to slow the fill rate, we would work two shifts. Apparently it was cheaper that way.

The first time I noticed anything unusual was when I found myself doing the night shift. We were almost at the point where the lake valley flattened out and the river flowed in. Already there were long tongues of dry land – peninsulas if you like – forming at the top. It was coming on dark and I was on the Cat. There were a few side-streams here from the braided river, and that meant a lot of willows to flatten. The other dozer on my side of the growing lake was further up to my left. We didn't use the scraper at night.

I was working on a line of willows and I just happened to glance across to my right. The water line was 50 yards away, then there was maybe twice that distance across a little bay to one of those little peninsulas. There was someone standing there on the shingle right at the end near the water.

My first reaction was that it was a fisherman keen to catch one of the big trout that were working the lake edges as the water rose. Boy, were there some big fish. I wasn't a fisherman but we were a bit naughty back then. Some of the guys would go spotlighting and spear them at night, or sometimes throw half a stick of gelignite at them. We had fried trout and salmon quite a lot on the job.

I worked on as the light faded. The figure was still there. I thought that because it was just standing and not moving, maybe it was someone fishing with a worm, just standing there watching his rod.

I last saw the figure when the sun went down. There was a bit of cloud so not much moonlight. I don't think I even thought about my fisherman again that night. Dropping trees under headlights takes a bit of concentration.

Next night I was back again, this time a bit further up the lake. The day crew had finished that patch of willows and I was shifting shingle, building quite a large boat harbour. The sun was just touching the mountains when I started.

I had probably worked for 10 minutes before I looked across the lake bed to see what the other crew were doing. As it turned out, they were doing virtually a mirror-image job over there. The powers that be were going to make this particular lake a real playground for the people.

Then I noticed he was there again – that lone figure standing out on the peninsula. I don't consciously remember thinking that anything was wrong. Let's face it, people do strange things. This figure was just standing there.

I was a bit closer now, probably 100 yards away, but the light was going. I looked around for a car. The roads were shingle, of course. There weren't a lot of places to park that I couldn't see from where I was on the dozer. No car.

Of course fishermen are like golfers, they walk for miles. I knew that even then. I just got on with the job.

About 7pm we usually shut down and had a bit of a smoko. Roger, the other dozer driver and I were both working on this particular harbour basin, and when time rolled around we shut down, grabbed our thermos flasks and met up for a break.

We climbed up on top of the shingle mound, which was about 10 or 12 feet high. I poured my tea and rolled a smoke. The moon was full and it was one of those beautiful clear high-country nights.

I was amazed to see that the fisherman was still out on the spit. I pointed him out to Roger. He'd seen him the day before as well.

'Don't think he's fishing,' said Roger. 'Hope he's not a bloody suicide merchant. Be a week before the water gets over his head at that rate.'

It was a bit of a tasteless crack but we both laughed. We sat and told stupid jokes until it was time to get going again.

At one stage I had to do a sweep run from what would be the entrance to the boat harbour right down to the water. There were a few big rocks that needed moving in case the *Queen Mary* ever came to dock in our little harbour.

It was a bit of a waste of time in my opinion, but the boss had said do so I did. As I clanked down towards the water, doing a shallow scoop and rolling a few goolies in front of the blade, I got within 50 yards of our mystery man. I realised suddenly that the figure wasn't dressed in men's clothing. It seemed to be wearing a wide coat or dress and its hat was a sort of bonnet-type thing.

Scotsman, I thought, half-expecting to hear the skirl of the pipes over the sound of the diesel.

I did about four or five runs down from the harbour to the water as the figure just stood there. I was tempted to drive up and ask if everything was all right. The water was probably only four feet deep – no trouble to the big Cat.

On my last run I decided I would do it, but when I was all ready I looked up and the figure wasn't there.

I was disappointed in a way. There were no car lights – but we wouldn't have heard a car engine over the roar of the diesels.

When we stopped for our next smoko I asked Roger if he's seen our mystery person leave. He said he hadn't. I told him I thought it was Scotsman in a long coat or a woman, because of the bonnet thing.

We finished up at dawn and headed away back to camp and our beds as the sun came up .

The next night we were further up the lake working in the picnic areas, scraping out carparks and access tracks. Looking towards the lake, I could see our figure was back. I never saw it arrive, although I'd sort of had my eye on the peninsula since I'd arrived. There was nothing, then there was.

'I'm going to go down,' I told Roger at first smoko.

'I was telling Fletch about it,' said Roger.

Fletch was one of the old-timers in the area. He'd been born not far away and had worked as a roader, rabbiter, musterer and all sorts of things before he'd got into dam building.

'What'd he have to say about it?' I asked.

Roger mumbled something.

'What?' I asked again. We were all a bit deaf in those days because of the machinery and I thought I'd misheard him.

'He said it might be a ghost,' Roger said again.

I just about dropped my cup.

'He says that last century a woman drowned trying to cross the river about here,' Roger went on. 'She was buried somewhere along the bank. Floods apparently took the gravestone. No one knows where the grave is any more. Maybe it's her.'

Ghosts! I couldn't believe what I was hearing. I got to my feet.

'I'm going down there to see whoever it is face to face.'

I marched off towards the lake. In the back of my mind I had the thought that maybe Roger and some of the guys were setting me up.

I was halfway down the spit when I realised that the figure wasn't there any more. I stopped and sort of squinted, but there was enough moonlight for me to see that there was definitely no one there.

I turned around and trudged back. Roger was standing there waiting.

'Nothing.' I said.

'What's that then?' he said, pointing back the way I had come. I looked and there was the figure standing where it had been before.

'But it wasn't there when I got close,' I protested.

'It was there all the time,' Roger said.

Well, if it was a joke, it was bloody good acting on his part. He was as pale as a proverbial ghost himself.

'You walk down and I'll watch from here,' I suggested.

'Not on your life,' Roger replied.

I tried to persuade him but he wouldn't budge. In the end I left him watching and went down again. This time I never took my eyes off the figure. I slipped and stumbled over the shingle, but I never once looked away.

I was probably 30 feet away. By then I could see it was a woman. She was facing away from me, looking down the lake. She had on a bonnet and a long dress with a wide skirt and a shawl around her shoulders. She seemed as solid as someone you would pass on the street.

Then, as I took two more paces she just went transparent, sort of dissolved – just gone.

I was totally stunned, but I had the presence of mind to walk backwards away from the end of the spit, and when I did, when I'd gone maybe those two or three paces, she was back again. I did it again and the same thing happened.

Then I admit I got the wind up and I walked very quickly back to where Roger was standing. I told him what had happened. He said she had never moved and had not vanished.

'What do we do?' I asked him.

'About what?' he replied.

'Our ghost lady,' I said, annoyed.

'There is no ghost lady,' said Roger.

I pointed down at the figure standing there in the moonlight.

Roger was shaking his head. 'Phil, there is no ghost lady. No one will believe us.'

He was probably right. I had some leave owing, starting the next day. Roger and the other guys finished off that project and a while later we were on to the next.

I didn't go back to that place for 30 years. It's now a top camping, boating and fishing spot and the spit the ghost lady had been on is long gone, under 20 feet of water.

I've thought about it every so often. Was the ghost lady the woman who drowned there? If so, why had she suddenly appeared? Official policy generally was that when areas were flooded, known gravesites were exhumed and the remains moved and resettled with all due ceremony.

Did the fact that her grave had been lost under the water mean she couldn't return to her resting place? Had she been caught in a kind of limbo?

I've often wondered if she found peace. Roger's long dead, and I've never told anyone this story before. Sort of feels better that I finally have.

Granddad's Tobacco Tin

It is my basic contention, as outlined in the introduction to this story collection, that ghosts don't travel well. Can they in fact travel at all? This story was passed on to me by an old acquaintance and it suggests that given the right circumstances (or people) they can.

It was 1969 and I was due to go back to Vietnam to rejoin my old outfit who had gone there some four months earlier. I'd broken my leg in a rugby match playing for the army and my rehabilitation had taken a while.

Two nights before I was due to leave I went home to see the folks down at Rotorua. They had a big do for me and it was just before I headed back to Auckland that my grandfather called me aside. We had a bit of a talk. He'd been a soldier and he was proud of me and of the army. Anyway, he reached into his pocket and took out his old tobacco tin.

I knew that tin well. Granddad had been in the Maori Battalion and the tin had been made up by a mate of his who was an engineer and given to him before they sailed to Europe. It was actually made of steel and it was quite heavy. The battalion crest had been engraved on it. Granddad was proud of that tin. It had been polished smooth through everyday use for 30-odd years. Now he was holding it out to me. 'It got me through my war, Johnny. It'll help you get through yours.'

I didn't want to take his precious tin away from him but I knew that if I didn't, it would hurt him deeply. I thanked him, we hugged, and then I was on my way north.

So it was that Granddad's old tin went with me into the jungle. Because cigarette papers are hopeless in the wretched damp of the Asian bush, I used to smoke American tailor-mades. You could buy them anywhere and they were cheap. I used to get a soft pack of Marlboro, slit one side and put it in my tin. It kept them from getting crushed and kept them dry.

The outfit I was with was the 13th Mobile Field Laundry, which was a standing joke. We didn't wash dirty laundry – we caused it. We spent a lot of time in places where sane people didn't really want to be. And there were not a lot of sane people around, certainly not in our lot.

We used to have a whole lot of tactics and techniques to survive in what was a very nasty place that had an equally nasty war going on in it. One of the more obvious things we did when we were overnighting in the bush, which was every night it seemed, was to create a bivouac camp. Its structure is important to my story, so here's how it went.

Imagine a series of concentric circles. The outside perimeter was where our sentries were positioned. A few metres inside that we would have another circle. This one was a track rough-cut through the jungle. The jungle was so thick, like a hedge, that even a two-foot wide-slash through it was like a highway. We could walk the perimeter track in complete darkness, just fingers touching the bush. On the inside edge of the track we had our individual bivvies, each right at the edge of the track. Inside us again was another circle. This was where the radio man, medic, sergeant and lieutenant set up their bivvies. There were a lot of other things but that was the basic set-up.

When it was time to set up camp, some were designated sentries and went on watch while the others set up their individual bivvies, then the sentries came in to do theirs while others went out on sentry duty. We each knew the drill without even thinking about it.

This afternoon I was on sentry first. I dropped my pack on the side of the track and pushed out to stand guard, while those behind completed the circle, cut down just enough green on the inside of the perimeter track to allow a scrape (small trench) to be dug for cover and set up the bivvy. Our bivvy kit was a tent fly or poncho, a mosquito net and a groundsheet. When it was done, a blanket or bedroll was laid out, a ration pack opened and that was that. Home sweet home.

We used to patrol for up to two weeks on the trot, which was a long time in the bush. You'd get tired, get jungle rot, crook guts and make mistakes as your ration of sleep grew shorter and shorter.

This night, when I was relieved, I went back to where my pack was and set up my Claymore mine (we each carried one) three feet over the perimeter, pointing straight out. I ran the wire back to my pack, covered it with leaves so no one would trip themselves, attached the firing mechanism and started setting up my temporary bedroom. It was full dark by the time I had finished. I didn't dig a scrape. I was tired and it was raining, as always. Anyway, we hadn't had any action with the enemy the entire time we'd been out. Things were pretty quiet.

I was lying back on my groundsheet when I suddenly got a strong feeling that I should dig a scrape. I don't know why, but I had this feeling and I was superstitious enough to think I should follow my gut, no matter how tired I was. I rolled off my bed, grabbed my trenching tool and start digging about a foot behind the bivvy.

Thinking about it now I realise it was more than a feeling – it was an outright compulsion. I dug like a terrier, kneeling there in the pitch dark, doing it all by feel. That night I made a really deep hole – the deepest I'd made all tour.

When I finished I was knackered. I rolled back onto my bed, took off my boots, then picked up my cigarette tin and took out a smoke. The tin felt warm and smooth. There was always something almost calming, soothing about rolling it in my hands. I carefully put the tin into my nearest boot; that way I could find it in the dark. The tin, that is, not the boot. I could find those by smell.

I checked that my mossie net was tucked under, checked that my M16 was by my right side, and that it was cocked, locked and ready to rock, as the Yanks used to say. My Claymore trigger was on my left side. All done. I closed my eyes and went to sleep. It really was that instantaneous. Even today, years later, I can still do that: just close my eyes and go to sleep.

I don't know exactly what woke me, but something snapped my eyes wide open. It was absolutely pitch black. In the bush the sun doesn't get down to the jungle floor during the day, and neither does the moonlight. But there was a light and I sat up blinking.

Three feet away from me, sitting on the track as plain as day, was Granddad. It was like he was glowing, but he wasn't. He was just there and I could see him as if were in daylight. All around was blackness.

It was a cardinal rule that you didn't talk in the bush, especially at night with the enemy about. Granddad was shaking his head, frowning at me. Then he raised his right hand, index finger extended, and moved it from side to side. It was a gesture that was very familiar from my childhood – a definite sign of disapproval.

I wasn't scared at seeing him; I was just sort of dumb-struck I guess. But I knew it meant something was wrong. I started to pull my boots on. It would soon be time for me to go back on sentry duty anyway. I didn't once take my eyes off the old man, who had by now stopped wagging his finger and was nodding. I pushed my tobacco tin into my breast pocket and buttoned it. I was just wondering whether to wake the others when the decision was made for me. It was about then that the first grenade exploded out beyond the perimeter.

I grabbed my M16, kicked my way out of the mossie net and rolled into my scrape, reaching back for my Claymore trigger. There was a burst of fire, then a machine-gun started away to my left.

There's nothing sweeter to the ears when you're in trouble than the racket a machine-gun puts up. Our second one off to my right was also in action. There was AK fire everywhere; the rounds were smacking through the trees above me. One went *viiiip* past my ear like an angry bee. I pushed my head closer to the ground. The smell of the stinking mud was comforting.

From the sound, it seemed we were under attack from all around. I was holding my fire until Smitty, who had been on sentry out in front of me, came slithering down his crawl-back. If I'd started shooting in the pitch black there was good chance I would have got him. I thought the first grenade might have been tossed at him.

'Okay!' Smitty was yelling as he fell into his scrape. We both cut loose on full auto with our M16s.

Mag change, re-cock, then I pressed into the dirt waiting. Soon we were away again – it seemed to go on for ever.

I heard the grenade land rather than saw it. It hit the top of my bivvy and fell a foot away from my scrape. I pulled back and remember pushing my face into the dirt of my trench. I pushed my hips down, pushed everything down.

Bang! Then everything went black.

I woke up I don't know how much later. Smitty was screaming for Lodge, our medic. There was still firing, but not much. I realised that Smitty was in my scrape with me – in fact basically sitting on me. He had his M16 held one-handed and was firing into the bush. His left hand was walking over my face.

'Where are you hit, mate?' His voice was coming from a long way away. It was like I was hearing him through cotton wool.

'Don't know!' I was shouting back. Then Lodge was crawling in to join us. 'Get off me!' I remember yelling at them both.

Lodge got me out of my scrape and pulled me back into the centre.

'Where are you hit?' he asked.

'Head!' I said, because that was where I was having problems. Everything else felt okay.

Lodge ran his fingers over my head. 'Bleeding from the ears, but no wounds.'

'I'll go back to my scrape.'

'Na!' he yelled. 'It's over. We caned them.' Somewhere a long way off someone else was calling for a medic. Lodge left, dragging his little pack behind him.

Nothing else happened that night. In the morning we did a tally-up. I still couldn't hear properly. Lodge reckoned the grenade had done my eardrums and it turned out he was right. But I could function okay, so I packed my kit and got ready for dust-off. But a soldier who can't hear is no good in the bush. 'Okay in the artillery!' one of the boys suggested kindly.

Anyway, there, right beside my deepest-ever scrape, was the foot-deep crater made by the grenade. The end cap of the grenade was sticking out of the side of my pack: I've still got it as a souvenir.

The Viet Cong lost 11 men and three women in that attack, and who knows how many injured. We had lost one man – one of the sentries. Another was injured with gunshot or grenade shrapnel to his shoulder, and then there was me. The dead man and we two injured went out by helicopter. I was back in hospital in Auckland three days later, my army career over.

Unfortunately it was a little more serious than ruptured eardrums and I have had a hearing aid in my left ear ever since. My right, which was nearest to the grenade, is completely useless. But at least I was alive.

While I was in hospital I found out that Granddad had died in his sleep while I was in the bush. How had his spirit found me that night? It must have been him who made me dig that deep scrape. He was the wise old soldier who knew that, next to his rifle, the trench is the soldier's best friend. I have no doubt that pit in the dirt saved my life. If I hadn't made that scrape, I'd have been lying there on top of the ground when that grenade hit and I would have been history.

I have never seen Granddad's ghost again but I still have his tobacco tin. I still love the smooth warm feel when I rub it. I have two sons, neither of whom is a soldier, but a nephew is thinking of it. Maybe in time his uncle will give him a gift …

Waka in the Mist

I heard this tale one night in a fishing lodge on one of the North Island's most famous trout rivers. There were half a dozen of us, all friends, all mad keen fishermen enjoying our annual boys' week away.

We would thrash the water (reasonably skilfully) to a frenzy every day. In the evenings we would return to the lodge with tales of the denizens of the deep that had or had not got away. We would eat the huge rich meals prepared by an internationally acclaimed chef, then sit and drink good liquor as we yarned the night away. Each morning we would drag our bleary-eyed bodies out of bed in eager anticipation of another glorious day on the river. It was a paradise that only an angler can ever know.

One night one of the group, a man we shall call Terry, told us a tale of his most unforgettable fishing expedition. It was a story that none of us is ever likely to forget.

I was working in Auckland at the time for a big US-owned corporation. A couple of the big-shots from New York were coming over, ostensibly to look at the New Zealand operation. Off the record, it turned out the only thing they were interested in was the trout fishing. Bud and Al were angling nuts and, as major shareholders in their company, they regularly used the excuse of checking their worldwide subsidiaries as an opportunity to fish.

I was a junior executive and it was my job to pick up the 'big boys' on Thursday afternoon off their flight from Los Angeles. Imagine my surprise and delight when I saw the rod cases with their luggage. We completed the introductions, loaded the car and headed back to town. We hadn't even got out of the airport carpark when they started.

'Say, Terry, you a fisherman?' asked Bud. Of course I answered that I was.

'Great!' said Al. 'What do you have planned for this weekend?'

There was a wedding that I really didn't want to go to and I grabbed the opportunity. My wife was going to be most displeased, but duty called. 'Nothing much,' I replied.

We were away. I got a briefing between the airport and downtown. They had done their homework and knew exactly what they wanted. I delivered the pair of them to the general manager and went to my office to fix things.

On Friday night, after the dinner and cocktail party in their honour,

WHERE NO BIRDS SING

Bud, Al and I set off for Taupo. I'd borrowed the general manager's Range Rover. He wasn't a fisherman and was delighted that I was entertaining our guests. The wagon was chocka with gear. I'd been told that the trip was a 'spare no expense' expedition that was coming out of the promotional budget. I had the boss's company gold card and his blessing to see that our guests wanted for nothing. Yahoo!

We grabbed a few hours' sleep in our motel and at first light we were down at the dock to pick up our charter boat. It took us five minutes to stow the gear and we were away. Gone were the thousand-dollar suits and the razors. Bud and Al were in jeans, check shirts and sneakers, complete with unshaven jowls and silly grins. The first beer was popped before we were 100 metres offshore. This was going to be a great weekend.

We trolled for a couple of hours and landed some good fish. We kept a five-pounder for lunch and had it barbecued in foil on a little beach, with salad and chardonnay. No trout ever tasted better.

Back on board Bud vanished below and came up with a rod tube and fishing bag.

'Let's get serious now, fellas!' he said as he started assembling a seven-weight Sage set-up that probably cost a month of my salary. Al used a state-of-the-art Hardy rig that was no doubt priced accordingly. My old unnamed vintage rod was a Volkswagen in a garageful of Rolls Royces and Bentleys.

Our skipper, Noel, took us in parallel to the shore and we could see big fish cruising the shallows. There was a bit of discussion on what flies to use. Noel had a good selection of local favourites. Bud, Al and I rigged up and we started fishing. The boat was ideally set up for fly fishing, with no rigging or such to get in the way of the back cast. Bud was in the bow, I had amidships and Al was in the stern. Noel switched off the big diesel and went to a little 5hp outboard that just nudged us along at a snail's pace.

Well, I have to say, the fishing was exceptional and my two companions were better than good at it. Their casts were long and clean. There was no trick to it: pick a cruiser and lay the dry fly on the water in front of the fish.

At one stage all three of us were playing fish. Noel was kept busy with net and camera. It was pretty much catch and release. Another nice five-pounder was kept for dinner and the rest were photographed and dropped back. That included a couple of real trophy fish that I would have considered keeping. Not so our American friends. The photograph and the memory were all they wanted.

It was exhilarating stuff. We were all using pretty light tippets because the lake surface was calm and the water gin-clear at the edges. We all got broken at times by big fish but it didn't matter at all. It was great to hear these high-powered Yanks laughing and fooling about like a couple of kids at a picnic, which it was.

All in all, we took 46 fish between us before the wind came up. Noel suggested we troll to our anchorage for the night, a little bay on the northern side of the lake. We caught another three good fish before we nosed in to shelter.

Dinner was hot smoked trout as an appetiser, followed by fillet steak, foil-roasted potatoes and salad, all washed down with good wine. True to type, the Americans produced cigars and we sat watching the sun go down, drinking port in the director's chairs that Noel produced from some hidey-hole below.

The talk was all fishing of course. Bud and Al told us about some of their expeditions. They had fished all over the world: salmon in Alaska and the Scottish Highlands; bass in the US southern states; trout in South America; barramundi in Australia; the torpedo-fast bone fish in Venezuela. They both agreed that on this, their first expedition to New Zealand, they were in trout paradise.

The boat had sleeping accommodation for six. We soon bunked down for the night as it had been a big day and we were knackered. There was a bit of wind and the motion of the boat soon rocked us to sleep.

I guess it must have been three or four in the morning when I heard a voice.

'Hey, you guys, look at this!' It was Bud, whose bladder had driven him from his bunk. 'Guys! Come and check this out!' His insistence dragged the rest of us from our warm beds.

There was a light mist on the lake but the moon was bright and we could see reasonably clearly. Certainly plainly enough to know what it was we were looking at.

There were four of them and they were perhaps half a mile away, moving past us, heading up the lake towards Kinloch.

'You've got a crazy canoe club here!' muttered a sleepy Al. 'This time of the night? It's three in the morning!'

Bud was shaking his head. I looked at Noel. He looked at me.

They weren't just canoes. I wasn't a scholar, but I knew a waka when I saw one, and here were four of them. All the canoes had the distinctive high bow of the Maori war canoe. They were long boats – there must have been 20 paddlers in each.

'Listen!' I think it was me who said it; I'm not sure now.

We could hear them faintly. It was a rhythmic chant just on the very edge of our hearing but it was there. Noel went to the wheelhouse and came back with binoculars. He looked for a moment, then he handed them to Bud, who was nearest. Bud in turn handed them to me. I adjusted the focus slightly and there they were, sucked in by the magnification. The picture I got was bright and clear because of the light-gathering characteristics of the glasses.

I could see the paddlers bending their backs, the blades of the paddles flashing wet in the moonlight. I was too far away to see the features of the individuals, but I could clearly see their naked torsos gleaming in the moonlight. The boats were definitely waka. I could plainly see the tall prows.

After a minute I handed the glasses to Al and looked back at Noel. He looked puzzled and a little uneasy.

'Crazy guys!' said Al, holding the glasses out for whoever wanted them. Noel took them again as the moon was shrouded by cloud. It stayed hidden for perhaps a minute, and when it came back the waka were gone. There was just the mist.

'You Kiwis are crazy guys!' repeated Al with a laugh. 'I'm going back to bed. There are fish to catch tomorrow. Then a plane unfortunately.'

'Me too,' said Bud, and he followed his partner below deck.

'Well?' I asked Noel.

He shook his head. 'I've been fishing here all my life, Terry. I don't know.'

'Is there a festival or something coming up?' I asked. I was groping for an explanation. What were four waka doing out on Lake Taupo in the middle of the night?

Noel shook his head again. 'Not that I know of. My people don't have four waka here at this time.'

I guess until that moment I never even considered the fact that Noel was Maori. 'Have we just seen a legend come to life?' I asked.

'Maybe,' he said, pushing the binoculars back into their case. 'Maybe. Anyway, it's time for bed. We've got fish to catch in the morning.'

Apart from a couple of mentions of the canoes over breakfast, and yet another good-natured comment about 'crazy Kiwi canoeists' when I farewelled our two well-satisfied fishermen at the airport that evening, I've never heard the four waka mentioned again, and I've never talked about them since.

Who's Sleeping in My Bed?

The narrator of this tale moved from a family home into a small ownership flat several years ago. Margaret suspects that the former occupant objected to her presence for a time.

I moved into my lovely sunny little flat in the late 1980s. It was a delightful spot and I was very happy with my choice.

There were no problems those first few months. The neighbours were nice, particularly Rebecca, the woman who lived in the adjoining flat in our little mini-block of two. She had known the former occupants of my flat well.

She told me that they had had a pleasant relationship, at least to begin with. Then, possibly unfortunately, Rebecca began to get on with the husband, Bill, better than with his wife, Mary. There was never anything going on there between her and Bill, Rebecca was quick to tell me. It was just circumstances really. Bill had cancer, and was home during the day. Mary had a part-time job and did a lot of charity work, so Rebecca, who was a widow and who didn't work, saw a lot of Bill.

She would drop in every day and quite often, if Mary was out, she would make their lunch. They also talked a lot about life and death.

Whether the decision to move was based on a little, or a lot of jealousy from Mary because of Bill's friendship with Rebecca, we will never know. If I am to be at all philosophical about it, I know that a friendship between male and female, particularly when one is married to someone else, can be a very difficult and threatening thing for the partner. Three's a crowd.

Anyway, according to Rebecca, when Bill and Mary moved out and across town, Bill really didn't want to go. But he was pretty sick at the time and he didn't have the energy to object too strenuously to his wife's demands. They moved out and that was the last Rebecca saw of Bill.

Mary made it plain before they left that she would prefer it if Rebecca didn't come visiting. She said that Bill would not be receiving visitors, 'because of his failing health'.

Rebecca felt a great sadness that things had turned out 'that way' in the end. From the time her neighbours moved out, she made it a point of keeping an eye on the death notices in the paper. I suppose we all do at a certain age anyway.

I had been in the flat for about three months, when Rebecca came in crying. She told me that Bill had just died. Rebecca went to the service.

It was probably a week or so after Bill's death, that my only ever supernatural experience took place. I was in my bed, sound asleep, when I awoke to feel the mattress moving. It was as if someone had grabbed the side of the mattress and was lifting it, trying to tip me out of bed. The movement wasn't violent but it was steady. The edge of the mattress was coming up five or six inches.

I could feel a presence in the room. It was very strong. Now, I'm a Christian, and I know my faith is strong. Despite what was happening, I didn't feel I was in danger. I just started to pray quietly, but aloud, and the mattress fell back. The presence was gone.

I lay in my bed for a while, then got up and went into the kitchen to make a cup of tea. I was shaken, I'll admit, but as before, when I was in my bed, I didn't feel really in any danger. I eventually went back to bed, and even went back to sleep. I didn't mention what had happened to anyone the next day. I thought that people would think it was just imagination.

The next night the same thing happened. The edge of the mattress was raised, and I could feel the presence in the room. As before, I just prayed and the disturbance stopped and the presence was gone. Once again, I got out of bed and went to make a cup of tea.

The disturbances continued, not every night, but two or three times a week. I went to my church and prayed for whomever, or whatever was doing this thing.

I did tell some people eventually. I don't think any of them really thought I was crazy, eccentric maybe.

Now even before this happened, I had been planning to shift my bed to take advantage of the natural light from the window. When my son and daughter came around, we moved the bed. Perhaps it was coincidence, but I my 'experience' never occurred again.

It's ten years since the incident last occurred, and the bed is back where it was when I originally moved in. I half expected my visitor to come back, but he, she, it, never did.

Incidentally, Rebecca moved away a couple of years ago, but before she left, we worked out what could have caused my little brush with the forces of the unknown. We concluded that Bill, when he left the flat, didn't want to go. He knew he was dying, he and Rebecca had discussed that in depth.

His bed had been in the exact position mine had originally been. Perhaps when he died, Bill's spirit had come back to the place he had been most happy in his last months. When the spirit found someone else, namely me, sleeping where he used to sleep, he tried to get me to move so that he could lie down.

That's our explanation anyway. Eventually, Bill's spirit just moved on and peace returned to my little flat. Bill is at rest, and because of that, so am I.

Sanctuary Tree

This tale was told me many years ago by an old Maori gentleman I worked with at the Makarewa Freezing Works just outside Invercargill. Given my love for tall trees, I never forgot the story.

I was a young chap at the time this happened – about 20 or 21. My family lived on a farm on the East Coast. Most of my brothers – there were four of us – worked at various freezing works during the season and did a bit of bush work in the off-season. Some of the boys were married and so were our two sisters, and while the married ones didn't live on the farm, they were always home visiting.

We single boys lived in a whare behind the main house. Mum did all the cooking and the washing, and we helped Dad and Uncle Ed on the farm when needed.

The farm next to us was government land. The year was maybe 1948, and quite a few blocks in the area were being balloted out to returning soldiers. Rehab blocks they called them. Kip, the manager who had been on the place for years, came over one day and said he was off down south to manage some other government place near Invercargill. Told us that the new owner was arriving in a few days and to look in on him, see how he was going.

We were all sorry to see Kip go. He was a good bloke. We had a big party to send him and Kathy off to the southern lands. We were still recovering two days later when we saw an old Chev flatbed come creaking and groaning up the road that ran past our gate to Kip's old place. We gave the new chap half an hour, then Dad, Ed, my brother Simon and I walked up the hill to say gidday. We'd seen when he went by that he was the only one in the truck.

Boy, was he glad to see us. He was Pakeha, and only a couple of years older than me. Had a big scar down one side of his face. He told me later that he had been a prisoner of the Japanese a few years earlier and the scar was from a Japanese sword. His name was Clive. Dad and Simon and I gave him a hand to get all the heavy stuff off the truck. Clive told us that in a week or so his mother and father would be coming down with his wife and young daughter. He wanted to get everything sorted for them.

We invited Clive over for a meal that night and talked about a lot of things – the war, farming in the area, politics. It was another late night.

Over the next few days we caught up with Clive now and then. He was mainly working around the house. Kip and Kathy hadn't maybe been the best housekeepers in the country and the old place needed a bit doing to it. Clive put on new weatherboards, fixed spouting and did a bit of wallpapering and painting.

Simon and I were working with a logging gang 20 miles away so we usually caught up with Clive in the evenings over a beer. We picked some up at the pub on our way home. Clive was grateful; I don't think he had a hell of a lot to come and go on.

In due course his wife Sue and their little girl, Jenny, arrived. Sue was a nice-looking woman about my age. She was pretty quiet. We soon found out that she was a city girl and this was her first home in the country – she was a bit scared. She told us much later that she came from way down south in Dunedin and she'd rarely seen a Maori in those days, let along talked to one. But Sue soon settled into farming life and they were good neighbours. They had another child on the way before the year was up.

At the start of the killing season Simon and I headed off to the works down south and were gone for more than six months. When we got back home we got all the family news and local gossip from Mum.

It seemed Clive and Sue were finding things pretty tight. Clive was running sheep and cattle. He was milking three cows and feeding up about 20 pigs. On top of that, he was helping out on neighbouring farms and generally wearing himself into the ground. Sue was pretty pregnant by now but was working as a relief teacher at the school in the village.

Our first night home Simon and I took a few bottles and went up to see Clive and Sue. We sat with Clive out on the porch and had a chat.

'It's been tough making ends meet,' Clive eventually confided. 'I need to put an extra room or two on the house with the baby coming.'

'There's plenty of timber around. Simon and I'll organise that for you,' I said, never really thinking where a simple statement and offer of help would take us all.

'Thanks, fellas. I could sure use an extra pair of hands. But I can't pay you.'

We weren't looking for pay and we told Clive so in no uncertain terms. Both of us were chain butchers so we probably made more in a month during the season than Clive saw in a whole year.

'I was looking at cutting that stand up the back paddock rather than go into the bush,' Clive said. 'There's that big kauri surrounded by some totara.

If I felled them I'd be able to build the extension and some new yards and probably have a bit to sell. That kauri's pretty big, eh?'

Simon and I looked at each other. We didn't know how to put it. In the end it was Simon who blurted it out.

'Clive, mate, you can't cut those trees down, they're tapu.'

There was a long silence as Clive stared at us. In the end he shook his head.

'Tapu?' he said. 'I don't understand. What do you mean?'

'Call it cursed if you like. Those trees are important to us Maori. There are plenty more and we'll help you find them and bring them out of the bush. But those trees are special, mate. That's why they're still standing out there in the paddock.'

'Yeah, okay, Simon. But they are on my land, right?' came back Clive.

Simon and I nodded. There was no arguing with that.

'But they're sacred trees, Clive,' I said. 'If you cut them down, you'll be cursed.'

It was about then that Clive got angry, starting on about 'stupid bloody Maori superstitions'. Simon got angry in return. I tried to be peacemaker but without much success.

Looking back, there probably wasn't anything we could have done to persuade Clive that although the trees were on 'his land', they belonged to everyone. There was no law then that said he couldn't cut them down.

Before things got really bad I took Simon by the arm and literally dragged him back home. We told the old people what had happened. Mum and Dad both got upset. Uncle Ed was away visiting, which was probably just as well, because he was known by one and all to have a really hot temper when he got wound up. Ed was very much into spirituality and he would have had a real go at Clive.

'I'll talk to him tomorrow,' Dad promised.

True to his word, Dad went up alone the next day and spoke to Clive. He told him the history of those trees and why they are special to our people.

The story is that during a period of fighting between the tribes on the East Coast and those in the Central Island, a young Maori princess, our ancestor, was the only survivor of a massacre of a food-gathering party. Pursued by warriors from the attacking people, Hau ran for her life. As she ran, she prayed to her gods to save her so she could avenge her people.

She ran throughout the long day, staying just ahead of her pursuers, who she knew would do worse than kill her if they caught her. Weakening, she scrambled up a steep hill. The spears of the warriors were landing closer to her with every step she took. At last she could run no further, so she prayed as she climbed into the branches of a young kauri tree.

Hau's prayers were answered as the tree began to grow, raising her high above the warriors who soon surrounded it. They threw their spears up at her in frustration, and one lucky spear hit her. Knowing she was dying, Hau wedged herself into the branches of the tree so that the enemy would not get her body, and she died, her blood dripping from the tree. Below, the warriors took her blood and smeared it on their faces in victory. They had killed her. They had won.

Angry that they had failed Hau and angry at the warriors for their callousness, the gods then turned every warrior who had touched Hau's blood into a totara tree – and there they stand to this day, the totara circling the mighty kauri that towers above them. The tapu that was placed on these sacred trees has never been lifted.

Clive listened in silence to Dad, then just shook his head and said he didn't believe in fairytales. Dad repeated the offer Simon and I had made to get other trees for him if he left these alone. Clive nodded and said he'd think about it and Dad left, feeling pretty optimistic.

Mum, Dad, Simon and I went to town the next day. I was going to get myself a new saw and Simon was getting some bits and pieces. We were gearing ourselves up for bush work with our old gang, and for selecting, dropping and dressing out the trees we had promised Clive.

We stopped in town until late. Mum and Dad went visiting while Simon and I went down to the pub to catch up with a few of our mates that we hadn't seen for months. It was six o'clock closing of course, but we all ended up at someone's place for a bit of a party.

We didn't get back to our place until next day. As we came over the first hill into the valley it was Mum who saw the black Dodge. This was one visitor that no one wanted parked in their driveway.

The big black undertaker's hearse was parked at Clive and Sue's house and beside it was a black Chevrolet with POLICE on the side.

'Clive!' said Dad, and we all knew it was him.

We drove past our turnoff and on up to Clive and Sue's. Bob Darcey, the local constable, was outside with the undertaker and Uncle Ed, who had just arrived back home from up north.

'Good. We can use a few fit young men,' said Darcey as Simon and I got out of the car. Mum and Dad went straight inside. We could hear Sue crying and yelling.

What apparently had happened was this. Clive saw us drive off to town the day before and Sue had gone off into to the village school in their old truck shortly afterwards. Clive got his tractor and headed out the back of his place to the stand of trees. He'd obviously figured to drop as many as he could while we were gone. That way the argument would be over – simple.

We found Clive pinned under the trunk of the old man kauri. He must have been killed instantly. Simon, Ed and I refused to follow Bob Darcey's suggestion of cutting up the tree. Instead, we helped him dig under it so we could pull Clive's body free. He was pretty badly broken up.

After the funeral Sue never came back to the farm. It was resettled by another former soldier a few months later. Out the back the kauri was down, but even today it is still untouched on the ground and the totara are still standing. Today all of those trees are protected.

Funny thing was, days after Clive's body was recovered, a whole group of us, led by Uncle Ed, went back to the stand of trees to lay things to rest. I noticed then, and Simon did too, that when Clive had prepared to bring down the big tree, he had definitely known what he was doing. There was a big deep scarf cut to direct the kauri's fall away down the slope. Yet despite this careful preparation, that huge tree had in fact fallen uphill to crush him.

I have often wondered if we could have done more to prevent what happened to Clive. In my twilight years I have come to console myself with the knowledge that nothing would have stopped him doing what he did. Clive's Japanese captors couldn't break his spirit. He was a man who set his course and stuck to it, even if it killed him, which in the end it did.

Ghosts of the Living

If you're not dead you can't be a ghost – can you?

I'm a semi-invalid and I spend quite a lot of my time sitting quietly watching the world go by – reading, knitting and gentle little pursuits of that kind.

I come from a family that has had more than its share of ghosts and seers and the like. I am, if not openly sceptical, certainly not gifted (or afflicted) with all the second-sight/hobgoblin stuff and I regard myself as a pretty down-to-earth sort of soul, not at all given to flights of fancy. That's what makes all this a bit silly really.

I was sitting reading in my favourite chair one day when I sensed someone outside the window. I looked up to see Jean, one of my oldest friends, walk past the window heading towards the front door. I was alone in the house at the time because my husband Graham was away at bowls, so I called out, 'Coming, Jean,' got to my feet and went to open the door.

I know I'm not that quick on my feet any more but I can move around not too badly. I didn't hear any reply from Jean, so I called out again as I made my way to the door. I knew she was a little deaf. Imagine my surprise when I opened the door and found no one there. I looked around the porch, expecting to see Jean walking back to her car. There was no one on the path, and no car parked in our driveway or out on the street.

I went back to my seat shaking my head. I'm not senile yet; I wasn't dreaming; I wasn't on medication. Jean had definitely been there. When Graham got back I told him what had happened. He smiled and told me I was losing my marbles.

If ever God put a sceptic on this earth it was Graham. My husband, bless him, is an absolute and utter sceptic. I'm a Catholic by upbringing and inclination; Graham is an agnostic bordering on atheist, but a good man for all that. He told the family that I was due for the loony bin.

A bit later I phoned Jean to check on her. I wanted to ask her whether she had actually come to visit and to see if she was all right. I'd heard stories about people who had passed on who sent their spirit to say goodbye. Perhaps something had happened to Jean.

But no, Jean was fine, and no, she hadn't been to visit me during the afternoon. When I told her my story I think she was inclined to side with Graham and conclude that I was losing it.

Well, that would have been the end of it, but it wasn't. I was a bit unwell one morning a few days later and I decided to stay in bed for a while. Graham was washing the breakfast dishes and came into the bedroom to top up my teacup. The main bedroom opens directly off the lounge, and the kitchen goes off to the other side of it. Anyway, Graham topped up my cup and went back through the lounge.

Then I heard him call out, 'Hang on, coming,' and go into the kitchen. There was the clatter of the teapot being put down and then the sound of the kitchen door being opened. I automatically assumed that a visitor was coming so I straightened up the bed and wished I had put on some makeup.

I didn't hear Graham talking to anyone, but then I heard the door being closed. I figured that maybe it had been a child collecting for something. A minute later Graham walked into the bedroom and sat down on the side of the bed. He looked confused to say the least. He was normally unflappable, but at this moment he definitely looked a bit on the flapped side.

'You know you said you saw Jean walk up the path last week?' he asked.

I nodded. 'Yes, how could I forget? You tried to convince everyone I was going off my head,' I replied.

Graham just shook his head. 'Well, when I walked out of the bedroom after giving you a refill, I saw Jean walk past the window. I called out, went over and opened the door, and she was standing there for a second, then she just faded away in front of my eyes.'

Graham just sat there, eyes wide. For a moment I thought he was pulling my leg, but he wasn't. He was dead serious. For once the great sceptic was stumped. He couldn't disbelieve what his own eyes had seen.

I rang Jean immediately, just to make sure she wasn't playing some sort of game. There was no way she could have got back to her place on the other side of town in under 15 minutes.

Jean answered the phone. She was fine – never felt better. She hadn't been over to our place but was coming over later. When she arrived in the afternoon I was sitting in my chair and Graham let her in.

'She's wearing the same cardigan,' he whispered to me as he went to make us a cuppa.

I hadn't seen it before. 'Nice cardigan,' I said. Jean smiled. 'First time I've worn it,' she said proudly. 'I was just finishing it when you called this morning.'

That was several months ago. So far we are all still on the planet, and my sceptical husband is still trying to figure it out. Hallucinations, holograms, X-rays – you name it, he's tried it on, but nothing has fitted …

Home Sweet Home

This tale is unusual in the sense that it is not unusual. Many readers will probably have had this experience, or will know someone who has. Perhaps only a few have taken the steps that Jane and her husband Rob took to rectify the problem.

We found our dream home about three years ago. It was a large old house in need of plenty of TLC. This was something that wasn't going to be a problem. Rob is a building contractor by trade and I am an experienced decorator. The house was set on a 10-acre block just close enough to town and the price was right.

We didn't waste any time closing the deal. We decided to keep our existing home for a few months while we did the major work on the new place. We were living a few kilometres away at the time so we commuted backwards and forwards, Rob mainly at weekends and between other projects, while I went most days. We worked on the basis that as soon as Rob had done the structural renovations on one room, I would move in with the paint and paper. It worked well.

One hot weekday I finished the painting project I was on and decided to take a well-earned break. I was alone in the house and felt totally comfortable there. I always had. I made a cup of tea and went for a wander around the property.

Apart from a couple of initial glances around the outer grounds I had never really paid much attention to what was on the farmlet apart from the house and the immediate garden. There were plenty of trees, including a small orchard. This had been the homestead for a large farm at some time in the past so there was the usual collection of sheds down the back.

I walked down the back, tea mug in hand, to explore. There was an implement shed with an old tractor in it and a few unidentifiable pieces of old farm equipment. The old barn had a few bales of hay in it and next to that was a small cow byre with a weed-filled hen-house built onto it. A well with a windmill, a pigsty and a little hut or whare completed the schedule of outbuildings.

The whare attracted me like a magnet. It was in pretty rough condition. Boards were rotted and the spouting had fallen down. Several windows were broken. Curious, I pushed open the warped door and went in.

The room I entered had clearly been the living area. It was about 10 feet by 8 feet – small by any standards. There was an old formica kitchen table with three hard chairs, a couch and some built-in shelves. The wallpaper was old and yellow and was sagging and torn. There were two doors on the back wall. The one on the right was open and I could see the frame of a bed. I poked my head in, avoiding the spiderwebs.

The bedroom was a mess, the remains of bedding shredded by rats and mice. The single window was broken and rain had got in to rot part of the floor. There was a chest of drawers and an old free-standing wardrobe.

I noticed that the light fitting in the middle of the ceiling had been pulled half down and the bulb fixture was gone. The room felt cold – very cold and damp. I quickly went back to the living room and opened the door to what I assumed was the kitchen.

The kitchen was poky, like the bedroom. There was an old Shacklock oven, and a Zip water heater half hanging off the wall over a bench that was covered in old pots and pans. The sink was filled with straw where a bird had been nesting. The old pantry still had old jars and tins and packets on the shelves.

Another door opened into a cupboard that passed for a bathroom. There was room for a handbasin and a shower with a faded plastic curtain. That was it. I went back into the living room.

I decided this would make a good sleepout, or playhouse for the grandchildren. It was far enough from the main house to be private and it would be a simple enough job to fix it. Once the house was finished, Rob and I could soon knock the old whare into shape. What a bonus!

I had been standing there musing for a couple of minutes, my tea going cold in my hand, when I suddenly had a strange feeling. Something wasn't right. When I'd come into the main room the first time the air had been hot and stuffy. Now the living room was cold. I decided the cold must be coming from the bedroom and I went and pulled the door closed.

But the cold stayed with me so I went out into the sun and closed the outside door. I didn't think any more about it. I walked right around the little hut, noting the boards that needed replacing, the broken windows and bits and pieces before I wandered back to the house to clean up my paintbrushes.

Rob and I moved into our new home a month or so later and I got stuck into the finishing touches: new drapes, restored furniture from auction rooms and junk shops to complete the look we were after. It was an exciting and busy time.

I pretty much forgot about the whare and didn't mention it to Rob for several weeks. We were planning on getting some chooks and pigs and one afternoon and we went down the back to see what work had to be done to make the hen-house and the pigsty habitable for the livestock.

Rob had his notebook and tape measure and made a list as we went. It was then that I mentioned my idea for 'out of house' guest accommodation and he thought it was a good scheme.

We went to the whare for a look around. Nothing had changed. This was a fine summer's day – in fact very warm, thanks to El Nino. Once again the main room was warm and stuffy but the bedroom was as cold as ice.

'Maybe it's just damp rot,' Rob suggested.

We looked over the kitchen and bathroom, and when we went back into the living room it was as cold as the bedroom had been. We were both glad to get out into the sun again.

'It was like that last time I came here,' I said to Rob.

He shook his head. 'Strange, all right,' he said. 'We'll start on it once we get the hen-house and the pigsty sorted out. Possibly a burst pipe underneath cooling it down. We'll see.'

We carried on with all the other chores and forgot about the whare for another month or so.

Our daughter Kate, her husband Brent and their two children came to stay in February of that year. Peter and Sandy were exuberant seven-year-old twins. They lived in Wellington and had been city born and bred. Having a real farm, albeit a small one, to play on and explore was paradise for them. By then we had chooks and pigs, and a couple of yearling calves destined for the freezer. There were a couple of horses we were grazing for friends, and a dozen sheep. Our 10 acre block was a busy little place for kids.

'Can we play in the house down the back?' Peter asked one day.

'Okay,' I said. 'But be careful you don't hurt yourselves.'

'And don't break anything,' added Kate.

The kids vanished at a rate of knots while we adults settled on the wide verandah with a cold drink for a good uninterrupted chat.

It was perhaps an hour later when the kids came back.

'I'm cold, Mummy,' Sandy shivered.

'On a day like this?' Kate replied. 'You can't be cold.'

'I'm cold too,' said Peter.

Kate turned to me. 'I hope they're not coming down with something.'

It was then that I remembered how cold the whare was. 'Where were you playing?' I asked.

'In the little house,' said Peter.

'We were pretending it was our own house,' said Sandy. Then she ran off down the garden. 'I'm warm again now, Mummy,' she called over her shoulder. Peter was away chasing her.

Rob look at me with an arched eyebrow. I explained to Kate and Brent about the whare and how cold it was. We discussed it for a few minutes, then a bee-sting on Sandy's bare foot ended that particular conversation.

Rob's business was going full tilt for the next months. He was working every hour of daylight he could find and we didn't get around to repairing the whare. The promise was that we would have it fixed up by Christmas when the whole tribe were coming to stay.

One spring day a neighbour rang to tell me that a couple of the sheep had got through the fence and were in his back paddock. Rob was working as usual so I went next door to retrieve them.

We had a nodding acquaintance with our back neighbour, a retired farmer. In fact at one stage he had owned the property we now had. He was in his early eighties, a nice man, a widower – a bit gruff maybe.

Anyway, between us we got the strays back through the fence and he produced a hammer and staples to fix the wires. We talked easily enough and I mentioned what we had planned for the whare that backed onto his property. He nodded, then floored me with his next comment.

'Have you encountered the ghost yet?'

'Ghost?' I was absolutely dumbstruck. 'What ghost?'

'In the whare,' he replied. 'Young Maori fellow that used to work for the man who had the farm before me. Forty years ago I guess. Lived in the whare. Had a bit of trouble – his wife left him. He got pretty depressed and eventually hanged himself in the bedroom. No one has ever lived there since. They left it the way it was when he died.'

That night I told Rob the story. A few days later I was talking to my father, who is part Maori.

'I'll speak to Fred,' he said. Dad's brother was an elder at the local marae.

A week or two after I spoke to Dad he phoned on a Saturday and said he and Uncle Fred were coming up to see us. In due course they arrived, along with three other men whom I recognised from the marae. Two of them I knew were tohunga.

'We'll lay things to rest,' one of them said to me.

The men all went down the back to the whare. I wasn't part of the ceremony they performed there but I could hear them from the house. After a time they all came back up to the house where I had laid out a lunch for them.

'It'll be fine now,' said Uncle Fred.

'He's moved on to a place where he will be happy,' said one of the elders. 'He was a lost spirit. Now he is with his ancestors.'

After Uncle Fred and the others had gone I went down to the whare. The living area was warm. The bedroom was still damp, but the aching cold was gone.

Before Christmas the whare was transformed. Everything had been fixed. We put in a new bathroom with attached toilet, did up the kitchen, put a built-in wardrobe in the bedroom and a gas fire in the living room. We replaced all the old furniture and made it a really nice little spot for our visitors.

No one complained of the place being cold ever again.

The Dead Place

This tale was told to me by a former bushman and professional meat hunter. He was working in the central North Island when this incident occurred.

I was working for a forestry gang during the week and meat shooting at the weekends. It was a pretty full-on time. I'd come up from the South Island, where I had been shooting for a living, to help my brother with a forestry contract. I would have preferred to stay with the hunting but Larry needed some help. The contract was about halfway through.

Scott, one of the guys in the gang, was Pakeha and he was married to a Maori woman, Anna, who had family living right on the edge of a prime hunting area. The country was easy compared with what I shot down south, and there were plenty of animals to be had. In fact I was making more money on the venison than on the forestry work.

Scott was keen for some extra money too, so we got organised and used Anna's family's place as a shooting base. We would quit work on Friday afternoon, pick up Anna and the kids and drive up to her parents' place. I should say her mother's place really – her father was dead, but not gone (which I'll tell you about shortly).

On our first morning on the property Scott and I hit the bush early with our rifles and a packhorse each. The bush was too nuggety to ride, Scott said, so we just led the horses. We would leave them in a meadow when we got serious about shooting and pick them up when we were ready to load up and come out.

We were intending to stalk our way across a large terrace and head for the sunny slopes of the hills behind. I was looking forward to it. The whole area seemed like prime deer country.

We had gone about 200 yards into the bush and Scott was moving off at an angle to where we wanted to go. I'd never hunted with him until that time and I thought maybe his bush navigation wasn't working properly. I pointed the fact out to him.

'Na, Pete. We've got to go around the Dead Place,' he said.

'Dead Place?' I looked blankly at him. 'What the hell are you talking about?'

'Just that. A place where nothing lives and nothing goes into it. Big circle – maybe 200 acres. I've seen it from the air. We go around it.'

'What caused it?' I didn't believe what I was hearing.

'Dunno. Anna's people say it's to do with dead people. It's no go, mate.'

Great, I thought. Walking around an area that big was going to take time, and all because of some Maori superstition. Coming from the West Coast, I hadn't had a heck of a lot to do with Maori stuff because there aren't a lot of people on the coast and therefore not a lot of Maori. I had a couple of Maori mates back home but they weren't big on the old ways I guess. We'd often hunted and fooled around together, but never got into any of this stuff.

'See the edge of it?' Scott stopped and pointed off to our right. It was an edge all right. Within a metre or two the greens of the bush gave way to grey. Everything beyond was grey – the ground, the trees, everything.

I went closer and the horse I was towing threw its head up and whinnied. It pulled back against me harder with every step I took. I eventually stopped when I was about 10 feet from where the grey began.

The area under the trees was open: no fern, just grey logs and grey dirt. The trees were skeletons with no foliage, but they all hung with long strands of grey moss or something. It reminded me of movie scenes of trees in the everglades with all the ghost moss on them. It was eerie.

'See the deer tracks?' Scott was pointing down at where we were standing. There was a wide deer trail leading around the area. 'Even the deer won't go in it,' he added. 'Or the birds or possums. You saw what happened when the nag thought you were going to take her in there.'

I nodded. I didn't know what to say.

We started off again, following the deer super-highway that ran around the edge. It was a highway. Obviously on encountering the Dead Place, the animals were forced to skirt it. The trail was a metre wide and very easy walking, which was a bonus.

Scott was right about the birds as well. They flew in the normal bush, but I never saw one flying away to my right. 'This is weird,' I muttered.

'You said it. Been that way for hundreds of years they reckon. No one seems to know what's behind it. Anna's lot stay well away and so do I.'

'You believe in Maori ghosts and stuff?' I asked.

'Don't you?' he said. 'I've seen and heard things that can't be explained any other way, Pete. They say, "don't go there"; I don't go.'

We carried on and eventually we left the grey behind us. We left the horses grazing coarse grass in a little meadow and got serious. It was a good hunt. We shot five animals between us, rough dressed them and collected them with the horses before heading back. We looped back on the other side of the circle this time and it was exactly the same as before. A wide deer trail ran around the perimeter. We didn't see anything moving in the grey area.

After that first shoot Scott and I went back often as a team. I tried several times to get Kuini, Anna's mother, to tell me about the Dead Place. Every time she would just shake her head. 'Bad place, Pete. Dead people's place. Bad luck even to talk about it.'

That was all she would ever say, and to this day, almost 30 years later, I have no idea what the Dead Place is all about. I often thought of cutting through it when I was hunting by myself, but something always stopped me. 'Dead people's place': I remembered Kuini's words and stayed out. Why tempt fate?

The Walking Stick

This story was also told to me by Pete, the bushman and hunter who worked in the central North Island.

When my friend Scott and I visited his wife Anna's mother Kuini for our various weekend shooting expeditions, I usually bunked out in a whare behind the house. I shared it with Scott and Anna's son Ben, who was 11 or so at the time. Scott and Anna slept in one of the bedrooms inside with their baby daughter.

One night after dinner I went out to the whare and got into my bed. Ben had gone off to bed a couple of hours earlier. Anyway, just as I was settling down to sleep, getting ready for an early start into the bush, Ben decided he wanted to talk.

'Hey, Pete! Have you heard Granddad in the house?' he asked.

This was a pretty odd question, I thought, as his grandfather had died when he was only two. 'Your granddad is dead, Ben.' I replied, figuring there was no easy way to answer him.

'I know that!' he said impatiently, as if I were a dummy. 'He died when I was a baby.'

'So how could I hear him if he's dead?' I asked as gently as I could.

'Because he's still in the house. I've heard him.'

'What do you mean?' I asked. I couldn't believe where this was going. I mean, we've all done the ghost-stories-around-the-campfire bit over the years, but here I had an 11-year-old doing it to me!

'Mum says that Granddad's ghost is still in the house. He stays there so he can look after Nana Kuini.'

'Yeah, well, I guess that's possible if your mother says it is,' I said non-committally. Ben had floored me on this. What on earth was Anna doing putting these ideas into her young son's head? I decided I was going to have a word with Scott about it in the morning. But Ben had not finished.

'You can hear Granddad's walking stick tapping when he walks around the house at night.'

Well, that just about did it. 'Time for sleep, Ben,' I said. 'I've got to get up early in the morning with your dad.'

'Night, Pete,' he said and promptly went to sleep, leaving me wide awake.

Next morning as Scott and I sat in the bush taking a break I told him what Ben had said to me the night before. Scott sat nodding until I had finished. 'I've heard old Matiu walking the house off and on for years,' was not what I had expected to hear.

'Not you too!' I said.

Scott grinned. 'It's true, mate. First time I heard that tap ... tap ... tap ... I just about had kittens. Anna and I were living up north when her dad died. Came down for the tangi, then we went back. Anna used to come down and stay for two or three weeks at a time then after a couple of years we moved back here. I didn't really know that Anna knew about her father's ghost being here. She'd never mentioned it.

'Anyway, that first night I heard the noise coming right down the hall outside our room. I didn't know what it was then. Just a tapping noise. It stopped outside Kuini's room for a minute or two, then came tapping back and away towards the kitchen. I got up but there was no one there. I told Anna and Kuini in the morning. Kuini just smiled and said, "That was Matiu looking out for me. He's still here, Scott."

'I was stunned. I'd forgotten about the walking stick. Old Matiu had had bad arthritis for years and used the stick all the time. It was a real beaut. It had been carved specially for him by a friend many years ago and when he died it was buried with him.

'So there you have it mate. Since then I've heard him dozens of times. Kuini's comfortable with it and so is Anna, so I guess I've got used to it. In fact, I heard him last night.' Scott stood up and stretched. 'Let's go get us some beasts,' he said, and that was that.

I never slept in the house so I never got to hear the old fella make his rounds, but I've no reason not to believe Scott's story. I suppose a friendly ghost is the best sort to have around.

The Waterfall

The links between spirits and water is a phenomenon that seems to be common the world over. This tale was told to me by a woman from the East Coast of the North Island.

Much of my childhood was spent on our family farm in a remote corner of New Zealand. It was wonderful place to grow up. My father and uncle ran the sheep and cattle property. It wasn't large by local standards, and when a neighbouring property became available, Dad and his brother Cecil decided to buy it for extra grazing.

This new block of land provided an exciting extended playground for us kids. There was a beach and cliffs, but we were never allowed to go near the cliffs without one of the adults with us.

On the highest cliff top, right on the point, there was a hole in the ground – long and deep and almost covered by grass. One day when my brother and sister and I were on the cliff top with Uncle Cecil and Rewi, the Maori shepherd who worked for us, I pointed to the hole and asked Rewi what had made it.

Rewi told us that many years ago a famous warrior chief had been buried here. The tribe he belonged to had lived in exile in a pa above the beach, perhaps a mile further up the coast.

'The people had been living there for many years,' Rewi said, 'after they were driven from their homelands during the Land Wars. When the tribes made peace they decided to return home. They dug up the body of their famous ancestor and took him with them so he could be buried in his ancestral homeland.'

We kids all thought this was quite fantastic. The thought of digging someone up and taking them away seemed so macabre. We had never really experienced death other than farm animals and pets, but after this we all had nightmares for a while, which was hardly surprising.

I always steered clear of that place on the cliff after that.

Then one summer's night Rewi's family had friends visiting and he arranged a big hangi down on the beach in front of the old pa, which was just some trenches now, all covered in grass.

The hangi was put down just back from the beach, beside the stream that ran down from the bush behind the pa site. Where the stream dropped to the level of the beach there was a waterfall and a big pool. We kids had been swimming in the pool many times, and the day of hangi we three, Rewi's two daughters and the kids from the visiting people all swam there because it was safer than the beach.

As it got dark the food was ready. We had a big driftwood bonfire and all us kids were wrapped in blankets against the cold. There was a wonderful picnic atmosphere and we were allowed to stay up late.

We ate the hangi, which had mussels and fish, a sheep and a pig Rewi had caught in the bush a few days before. The adults had beer and there was soft drink for the kids. After the food we all sat around the fire and talked and Rewi told us stories about the people who used to live here.

'They built their pa out of big logs. It was strong, and when other tribes came to fight them they easily won their battles. All but one,' he added ominously. 'There was one battle in which they had to come out of the pa and fight here on the beach. They won, but they lost many warriors. The battle was fought over there.' He pointed towards the waterfall.

Everyone turned to look at the waterfall and the pool. The light of the moon had turned the water black and silver. We kids were wide-eyed by this time.

'They fought the battle on the night of the full moon,' Rewi went on. 'And you know, whenever there is a full moon you can see the ghosts of the warriors fighting and you can hear them.'

That did it for us. The moon wasn't quite full that night but we huddled in our blankets as close to our parents as we could, casting fearful glances at the place by the waterfall. That was the signal for our mothers to pile us onto the back of our old truck and take us home while the men stayed by the bonfire and drank their beer and undoubtedly told other stories not suitable for young ears.

This story had a profound effect on me and I resolved never to go to the beach at night, particularly when there was a full moon.

I was probably 20 or so when I came back to the farm from Wellington where I was working. Mum and Dad and Cecil and Aunty Marg still lived there. The other kids were all grown up or close to it.

Rewi had died, killed in a tractor accident years before. His wife Tanya and their kids still lived on the farm. Dad and Cecil let her stay in the house that she and Rewi had lived in for years in return for help around the place. The two daughters, Rangi and Tina, were at high school and still lived with her.

One hot night Rangi and Tina and their boyfriends Arch and Dingo

THE WATERFALL

invited me to go down to the beach for a barbecue. They had caught fish and gathered some mussels and pipis.

So there we were, the five of us down on the beach. I had almost forgotten the story that Rewi had told us all those years ago. It was only when were sitting around the fire eating our beautiful fresh fish and talking that I noticed that it was a full moon and the tale came back.

I didn't mention the story to the others. After all, I was 20. I was the mature one! But throughout the evening I couldn't help glancing down the beach to the waterfall, half expecting to see ghostly warriors fighting.

After we ate I decided that five was a crowd and I quietly slipped away to walk back up the track to the house about two miles away. I said my goodnights and left the youngsters to it.

At one point as I climbed the steep track up above the beach I stopped and sat on a rock to catch my breath and looked back below me. I saw the bonfire on the sand in the middle of the beach. The waterfall was at the end of the beach to my left.

My imagination was working overtime I guess, but I thought I could see shadowy figures in and near the water. There were indistinct grey shapes coming together then falling apart. Could I hear the sound of shouting, or was it the other four on the beach talking? The night was clear and calm, with just the sound of a small surf tumbling onto the sand.

Imagination! I scolded myself, quickly got to my feet and started back towards the top of the hill.

I stopped again when I got to the top. By now the beach was a long way below me. I squinted towards the waterfall but I was too far away. I could have sworn I heard the sound of shouting, but I quickly dismissed the thought again. The mind can play some good tricks.

By now I was a bit edgy though and I literally ran all the way back to the farm. Some of the track ran through patches of bush and every shadow seemed to have a life of its own. I kept my eyes straight ahead and sprinted through the dark places, barely able to see where I was putting my feet despite the bright moonlight.

I arrived back at the house wringing wet and puffing. Mum and Dad had already gone to bed. It was about midnight I suppose. I snuck a glass of Dad's whisky to calm my nerves before I had a shower and went to bed myself. Oh, the nightmares I had that night.

Next day I went down to Tanya's to see Rangi and Tina. I had managed to convince myself that the previous night had been all in my mind – the power of suggestion. The girls had just woken up and the first thing that

Rangi said to me when she came out on the porch was, 'Did you see them?'

'See what?' I asked.

'The ghosts!' she said.

'What ghosts?' I replied, my heart in my mouth. She's having me on, I thought to myself. She knew the story from her dad and she was winding me up. But she looked dead serious.

'After you left, we were just sitting there talking and we heard some shouting. We thought someone else had come down the beach, some guys. We thought if they were drunk there could be trouble, so we got our gear together and got ready to leave. Then we saw them along the beach by the waterfall. There were men fighting. Tina and I remembered Dad's story and we got out of there. We ran all the way home.'

Rangi looked terrible – she obviously hadn't had much sleep. Tina came outside about that time and she was nodding. 'It was scary, Del. It wasn't our imagination, it really wasn't. The guys saw and heard them too. They were as scared as we were.'

Dingo and Arch had stayed over, sleeping in one of huts behind the house. When they joined us, they confirmed what Rangi and Tina had told me.

'They were fighting all right,' said Arch. 'We could see them like watching an old black and white movie. All grey and sort of transparent, not solid looking. Boy, I'm not going back there at night again.'

He looked as if he hadn't had much sleep either, and Dingo was the palest Maori I've ever seen. 'Me neither,' he said. 'That stuff scares me to death.'

I went back to the beach a few times before Dad and Cecil sold the farm, but never at night.

Imagination? I don't think so. Not when all five of us experienced it. And it's not as if we had been sitting on the beach telling ghost stories or anything that night. While Rangi, Tina and I all knew the story from years earlier, the boys had never heard it before.

Rangi said that in fact it was Dingo who had first seen the shadows after they heard the sound of the voices. He'd said something like, 'There they are. They're fighting. Let's get out of here.' That was before he realised that they weren't flesh-and-blood people. He'd thought they were a bunch of drunken hoons from the town.

For months after these events I used to wake up in a cold sweat from nightmares about it. Twenty years old or not, I didn't feel so grown up after that.

Gerald's Road

This story is one that has not ended yet. It was told to me by a Maori friend who hopes that the people involved will seek a conclusion by communicating with those who can and will help – if they are asked to.

It all began about 150 years ago when members of my family sold quite a lot of their land to Pakeha settlers. They did, however, retain some prime pieces and set other areas aside as reserves. Throughout the entire area that my people had owned and still do own there are many burial grounds, and one of these is at the centre of this story.

In more recent years my immediate family reluctantly sold off one large piece of land. The problem was that a family member urgently needed a considerable sum of money and the only way to raise it was to sell off some land.

The land was sold to a Pakeha farmer who had been a neighbour of my family for many years. The relationship between him and my family had always been a good one. Gerald had been after that piece of land for years in order to install one of his sons on his own place.

The problem began when Gerald wanted to put a road through the new property to the house that was on it, shortening the route to his own home.

Now, Gerald had always been aware of our Maori traditions and had always abided by them. But one day he was talking to a kaumatua called Tama and told him where he was going to put the road. Tama said a very emphatic '*no*' and explained that he could not put the road through one particular place at the top of the cliff because there was a burial ground there.

But not doing so would have meant the route would have to be perhaps 20 or 30 yards further up the hill and maybe 100 yards longer. Gerald wasn't having any of it. He put the road straight through across the top of the cliff.

Sure enough, the man driving the digger found bones and the remains of cloaks and other burial objects, including some ornaments. He got quite a shock and wanted to quit the job but Gerald talked him into finishing.

When the road was through, Gerald went and reburied everything off to the side. He didn't tell any of our family about it, but some of them watched him from a distance. Some also said that they thought he took something, perhaps an ornament he found there. I don't know if that was true of not, but if it was, it could explain what happened later.

What I do know is that my family and the other Maori families who lived in the area were pretty upset by Gerald's actions. I think the hardest thing to accept for those of us who had known him for years was that he had ignored us, and our traditions, point blank for the first time.

But the general feeling in the community was that what goes around comes around, so life continued on as normal. Because the area was pretty small no one had a real go at Gerald, although a few people, including my father, did express their deep disappointment at what he had done. It was like water off a duck's back. As far as Gerald was concerned the land was his and he could do what he wanted with it.

One day about two years after the road went in Gerald was standing yarning to another kaumatua from the local tribe at the point where the new road crossed the cliff top. The kaumatua had gone up there to talk to his ancestors when Gerald had come along. The two of them were standing talking about everything other than the road and burial ground, when Gerald suddenly dropped down dead. There was no warning; his health to that point had never been a problem.

When the news got around some of the old people nodded their understanding. I was just a kid at the time but I still remember that line: what goes around comes around.

Once again life carried on as usual. It was a few years later, about six or seven I think because I was at high school, when Gerald's son David, the one who had taken over the new farm, also died. One morning he had just kissed his wife goodbye, as he did every morning, left the house and walked down the road to where it came across the cliff – and kept on walking. No one knows what made him do it.

Three years later on the same spot where David died, a driver delivering goods to the farm lost control of his truck. Somehow he managed to get out before it went over the cliff and destroyed itself on the rocks below.

It's been 15 years since Gerald's road was put in and there have been other accidents on those 200 yards of shingle. Certainly, all roads have a few incidents on them, it's just that there seem to have been a lot more there than on others in the area. The feeling is that it is just a matter of time before there is another death on Gerald's road.

Gerald's family still have the property. They know that things aren't right. Many of them choose to use the old road rather than Gerald's road. David's wife certainly never uses the new one.

GERALD'S ROAD

But what the family still haven't done after all these years is sit down and talk to the old people and ask how things can be put right. They can be put right very easily, but they must first ask. That is the important thing. They must ask for the help that is there for them.

The God Eel

Born and bred on the East Coast of the North Island, as a Pakeha in a predominantly Maori area, David thought he had a pretty good grasp of Maori superstition and legend. That was until he decided to go eeling where he shouldn't have.

My father was a school teacher, principal of a four-classroom school. Mum was a nurse who worked as the assistant to the district nurse. We were the only Pakeha family in the village and we'd been on the East Coast ever since I was a baby. At the time of this story I was 11 or so.

I guess when it comes to bicultural relationships I knew no other sort. I spoke Maori and had done all my life. All my friends were Maori – mostly boys of course; we weren't that interested in girls yet. It was a great lifestyle that I missed in later years. We had it all: bush for games, rivers and the sea for swimming, horses to ride, barefoot rugby and fishing.

Fishing and eeling were always our favourites. The local rivers and creeks teemed with eels, and there were snapper and cod in the sea, which was a 10-minute bike ride away. We were in kid heaven.

There was one place, though, where we weren't allowed to eel. It was on a bend in one of the creeks that ran around the end of an old pa site. The earthworks of the pa were all that remained, and they were high, at least to a kid – seemed like the rice terraces you see in photographs of Bali and places like that.

'That's where the special eel lives,' was the reply when I asked my friend Hemi why we never went there to eel. It was the perfect spot of course: close to the village, with a track right to it. We'd fish a hundred yards either side of the bend, but never right on it.

'It's a god eel, Davy. Tapu, very special,' Hemi told me the first time I pushed for more details.

I don't know if it's a Pakeha thing or not but I had trouble accepting the idea that one eel could be so special while the rest weren't. I mean, we were always catching eels and taking them to Hemi's Uncle Sam to smoke in his big smoke shed. Sam used to keep half of what we caught, and we had the rest to take home. Everyone loved Sam's smoked eel. Even today, 40-something years later, I have never tasted better, and I've been around the world a couple of times, sampling the local product wherever I was.

THE GOD EEL

Anyway, I just couldn't see why this one place and this one eel were so special. I really wanted to see it, maybe even catch it. I tried to find someone who had seen it, but among the kids no one had.

I suppose I should have let it rest, but I think I was a bit angry or something. I probably couldn't have come up with the word superstition at that age, but that was what I saw in them. I thought they were acting like kids (which they were, just like me!).

Looking back, I see now that I had had no problems up to that stage in going along with the other 'superstitions' my friends subscribed to. I think all kids live in a fairytale world and there's nothing wrong with that. Maybe I was just starting to grow beyond the gullibility of childhood. I don't know, but anyway I decided I was going to eel on the bend in the creek. I didn't tell my mates. I knew what they would say and someone would tell one of the oldies and I would be in trouble.

The creek was one of those deep black ones. We never went swimming in it. It also meant there were no places to cross except at the two or three bridges between where it came out of the bush and where it went into the sea.

I made my plans. I was going to go late in the afternoon, just as the sun started to get close to the trees. I wasn't going to go on the pa side, which is the side the village was on. Instead I was going to cycle up to the nearest bridge and down the other side and fish across from the pa on the outside of the bend. It was about a three-mile ride I suppose.

Deviously, I told mum I was going to Hemi's for tea and told Hemi and the others that I was staying in for tea and that my father had some jobs for me so I couldn't play late. I knew someone would see me on the bike but I figured that they'd think Dad had sent me on an errand or something.

My eeling line and hooks and sinkers always lived in the half sugarbag that I had on the back of my bike as a saddlebag. I wanted a real stinky bait to catch this big eel with and I knew just where to get it. There was a dead hare on the side of the road just down from the school, which had been there for three or four days – perfect.

After school I played with Hemi and Dan and the gang as usual, then just before the time we usually had tea I said goodbye to the others and went home and got my bike. I told Mum I'd be back before dark and took off. There was no sign of the other kids when I rode out of town.

The hare really stank. It had been pretty hot with lots of sun so things were wriggling. I had a piece of string so I tied it on the carrier and set off for the bridge. Then I saw Hemi's Dad, Ricky, coming my way in his truck.

He worked at the sawmill up in the bush. He tooted and waved as he went past. I knew he'd be wondering where Hemi was. I knew he would say something to Hemi but I didn't care. I was going to catch the big eel.

I pedalled faster as I crossed the bridge and I looked down at the water. It was so slow moving and so black. I think I felt a shiver pass down my spine, but I kept on going, pedalling faster still. There were no gears on the bikes we had back then, and just a chain brake.

I was puffing when I finally pulled off the road into the trees on the bend. No one could see me from the road unless they were really looking. I got the hare off the string and tried not to gag. I used my fishing knife, which was an old kitchen knife that I'd sharpened on Dad's grinder.

I opened my sack and got out my line. We didn't muck about when it came to catching eels: the line I had was genuine cod line, a twisted cotton or hemp, thick and strong, not nylon. It was wound around a stick that had one end sharpened so I could push it into the bank to secure it. My sinker was a great big nut off an old gold stamper up in the bush.

I had two hooks, both big long-shanked cod hooks and both really sharp. I had a piece of an old file in my sack and I kept the hooks in top shape. Sam told us to do that. 'Keep your hooks sharp and you'll catch more fish more quickly,' he was always telling us.

I worked the bait onto the hooks and then I pulled off plenty of line, pushed the stick deep into the bank and picked up the sinker. There wasn't room to swing the line because I was tight under the trees. Instead, I just made sure the hooks wouldn't snag me and threw the nut out like a cricket ball. I got distance, and the sinker vanished into the black water about mid-stream.

I squatted at the water's edge and washed the bait smell off my hands, while not leaving my hands in the water a moment longer than I had to. I don't know if I believed the story about the giant eel – all I knew was that the creek held a lot of eels and that some of them were very big. This part of the creek was particularly prime eel territory since no one else ever fished here.

I stood up and waited, half fearful that a car filled with angry Maori would come flying down the road. That, or I would actually catch the giant eel. I picked up the line and held it, waiting for the tell-tale double tug that signalled that an eel had taken the bait.

The sun was just touching the tops of the trees and the shadows were starting to get long. The sluggish current or weed dragged on the line and it sort of vibrated in my fingers, but no tug.

THE GOD EEL

I waited and I waited. The sun was half gone. It must have been 10 minutes and no bite. Now, that was unheard-of in our area. It was no exaggeration to say that in this creek, with the sort of tempting bait I had on the hooks, I should have caught at least two eels by now, probably more.

The splash, when it came, gave me the fright of my life. It was huge – bigger than any fish splash I have ever heard or seen. The water in the middle of the creek suddenly boiled and the line in my hand just took off. I burned my fingers as I tried to stop it, then it was gone and the piece of wood I'd wound the line around and stuck in the bank was flying past me. I grabbed at it and missed, almost slipping into the water as I did so.

It was gone, whatever had made the splash and the water boil, and my prized line had gone with it. I remember stepping back from the water, feeling quite shaken. I hadn't really seen anything but I felt it and heard it. I stood staring at the water but there was nothing. No more splashing, no sound. With the sun all but gone the creek was as black as tar, barely moving.

I'd had enough. I put my knife in my sugarbag, pushed the bike up to the road and set off for home, going like the clappers. It was not yet dark and Mum observed that I was home on time for once. I just went to my room. I didn't sleep very well that night: I kept having nightmares about tarry creeks and huge black eels.

Next day was Saturday. I got up feeling groggy from lack of sleep. I did my chores and wondered how I was going to get another fishing line. Hemi and Dan and the rest of us had planned on biking down to the beach to fish. The tide would be right about midday according to Hemi and he always got it right. Trouble was that the eeling lines did double duty for us all. None of us had fishing rods back then – it was always hand lines and I didn't have a spare one.

I had just finished feeding the chooks when Hemi's Uncle Sam came up the street in his old Vauxhall. He stopped and waved me over.

'Hey, Davy. You lose something?'

I looked at him, not having an clue what he was talking about. 'No,' I replied.

'Oh,' he said, 'then I guess this isn't yours.' He held up my fishing line. It was all neatly wound on the stick. The hooks were clean and shiny and the big nut was over the stick keeping everything in place.

'That's mine,' I said.

Sam handed it to me. 'Next time be more careful,' he said, and looked at me to see I understood.

I did. I nodded. Sam returned the nod. He was about to drive off when he stopped, a thoughtful expression on his face. 'Hop in and I'll show you something, Davy.' he said. 'Tell your mother you're going with me.'

I ran inside and told Mum I was going off with Sam for a bit and got in the Vauxhall. I didn't have any real idea what Sam was up to, but I knew it had something to do with what I had done at the bend in the creek. It was no surprise when Sam turned down the old pa track. When we got to where the track met the creek he stopped. He told me not to say a word, just to follow him.

As he walked Sam started speaking a Maori language I didn't understand. It was different to what I was used to. He motioned me along after him. I wasn't scared or anything but it was a bit strange. When we got to the place on the bend Sam stopped and began to sing. Again, I couldn't understand him. Some words, yes, but most of it went over my head.

As I stood off to one side my eyes were on the water. At first I don't think my eyes actually told my brain what I was seeing. The water was moving and this huge broad black head came to the surface. It came gliding towards the bank. Even today, I can't get the size of this eel sorted out in my mind. I'd seen big eels, lots of them. We'd caught a six-footer once. Its body was as thick as a big man's thigh.

I never saw the body of this one, just its head, and it was at least as wide as a workman's shovel, and the same basic shape. It was jet black, had big thick lips and black eyes that seemed to be looking right at me.

I just froze where I stood. The eel came right in to the bank and put its head on the grass by Sam's feet. Sam knelt down and touched the head, stroking it with his fingers as he sang to it. It was like he was patting a dog or a cat. The eel seemed to like it, the water behind it boiled, but I still didn't see its tail or anything. I just couldn't take my eyes off its head: it was so black and shiny and just huge.

After maybe a minute the eel slipped back into the water and was gone. A few minutes more and Sam stopped singing and stood up. He turned to me. 'I told it you were sorry.'

I just nodded. My throat was dry. I couldn't have said anything even if I had known what to say.

Sam gave a chuckle. 'No harm done this time,' he said. 'Look, Davy. The eel is very important to Maori. Long ago it was a special gift from the gods. To some tribes it is a god. We must look after eels.'

'But you eat them,' I said.

He nodded. 'Yes, that is the way of it. But we also protect them.'

'I don't understand,' I replied.
'One day you will. But no more eeling here. Okay?'
'Okay,' I agreed
'And don't you tell anyone about this – not your mates or your parents. This is between us. You are a good boy. I only showed you so that you will understand a little better why some things must be as they are and stay as they are.'

I never forgot those words. And I said nothing about what had happened to anyone. Sam didn't say another word about it either. I never saw the giant eel again, no matter how often I went to look for it – and I did go looking for it; I went to the old pa at least once a week for the next two years before we moved off the coast to the city. I still can't believe it was so big. But if it was ...

Des and the Dogs

The inhabitants of a small central North Island township had a solitary experience with a very special ghost, one that had an affinity with the township's many dogs. We'll call the township Tama.

I come from Tama, a small town in what many would consider to be the middle of nowhere. There's not much there. We have a pub, a store, a garage and about 30 houses. Most of the people are retired or work in the bush, on neighbouring farms, or are on the dole.

It's not a prosperous place, but it's home to a great little community. It's the sort of place where people definitely have to create their own fun, and we do.

As in many of the townships in the bush country, hunting is a way of life in Tama. Pigs are abundant, and never a week goes by without wild pork being on the menu somewhere in town.

My tale concerns a man named Des, who was regarded as the best pig man in the area.

Des had lived in the town from childhood. I don't think he had ever been further north than Hamilton, and once he went south to Feilding with the local rugby team. That was about the extent of Des's travels. Some say he had never seen the sea, and I can believe that.

Des was a bushman and had worked for a forestry company since he was old enough to swing a chainsaw. When he had done his week's labour in the bush he got his horse and dogs and went back to chase pigs. He rarely came home without one or two across his saddle.

Des usually owned four dogs. They changed as they got old, or ran foul of a mean-tempered Captain Cooker and had to be put down. But he always hunted with more than four dogs. As he rode through town on his way to his favourite hunting ground he would whistle up any dog that wasn't tied up. Sometimes he would leave town with 10 dogs trailing behind, yapping and snapping behind him.

The dogs loved Des and the hunting. How he controlled them we never knew, because Des always hunted alone. Just himself, his horse, the dogs and the big white-handled knife he always wore on a belt over his Swannie.

Des was a big man – some would say fat – and he was very strong. As

DES AND THE DOGS

kids we would see him drop his catch, often really big animals, off the horse, then pick them up, sometimes one over each shoulder, and carry them into his 'pig house'.

There he had an old bath with a fireplace under it. He would have water boiling in the bath, and the pigs were scalded and cleaned and hung from big hooks fixed to the roof beams. Sometimes he would have four or five hanging there.

The pigs were destined for some place up north. A man in an old Ford truck with a cold box on the back would come down just about every Sunday evening to Des's pig house and drive away with the weekend's catch. Some said that Des made more money from the pigs than he did from his regular job.

I was at high school. All the kids from town and the surrounding area used to catch the school bus for the long drive to Rotorua. Weekends to us were magic. We would do all the kid things, but we were always around when Des came back into town in the evenings with his posse of dogs and his catch. We would run alongside his horse and talk to him and admire what had fallen prey to him and his dogs. Des didn't say much; he'd usually just give us a grin.

One thing that did cause the occasional stir was the fact that some of the dogs that went into the bush with Des didn't come back. The pigs could be pretty ferocious. The word in town was that if you wanted to be sure you saw your dog again, you should tie it up on Friday night, because Des generally went bush early on Saturday morning.

Our house was at the opposite end of town from where Des lived, and I can remember often waking up to the sounds of Des's whistling, the horse's hooves on the shingle, and noise of a pack of excited dogs. Sometimes my brother Nathan and I would get out of bed and go to the window to watch, mainly to see who hadn't tied their dogs up.

Anyway, it was in my last year at high school that it happened. Des went into the bush on Saturday morning as usual, but this time he didn't come back. My mates and I had been eeling down at the creek and when we got home some of the men were getting organised to go and look for Des. Some of the dogs that had tagged along with him had straggled back into town, but not Des's own dogs.

Everyone knew that he had a bit of heart problem. He had been to the doctor in Rotorua a couple of times about it, and had been off work a lot over the past year. The feeling was that he had had either a heart attack or an accident. Sometimes in the past he had come back from a hunt torn up by a mean old boar. He never seemed to think the injuries were serious but to us kids they seemed pretty bad.

The men had torches because night wasn't far away. We kids wanted to help but Dad said, 'It'll be hard enough looking for Des, without trying to find a bunch of lost kids.'

He was right of course. The bush was pretty wild in places. So the men set off, led by the foreman from one of the forestry gangs in his ute. He had a radio telephone in the truck. The rest went on horses or on foot.

I guess it must have been nine or ten at night when we heard the police car come through town with its siren going. The nearest police station was 30 miles away.

Much later the men came back, and so did the police car, but there was no siren this time. We all piled out on the street. There was only one street light in town, between the pub and the store, and that was where we all gathered. When the ute came in we could see the shape in the back under a piece of canvas. We all knew it was Des. His horse and dogs were brought in a little while later.

They had found Des in a clearing in the bush, a big dead pig lying beside him, his dogs were standing guard. Apparently Des had killed the boar and dressed it out, then when he had tried to lift it onto the horse his heart had given out.

It was a big tangi. Everyone liked the quiet giant of a man. It was fitting that the last pig he had killed was put in a hangi for him. He had died doing what he loved and what he had done best.

Des's dogs had to be put down. They were one-man dogs, and in the days following his death they didn't eat, and became even more dangerous than pig dogs normally are. One of my friends got bitten by one of them, so there was no alternative. Dad and one of his friends did the unpleasant duty with Dad's rifle.

Things eventually got back to normal in town. I still woke on Saturday mornings half expecting to hear the sound of Des and the dogs.

I finished high school and moved to Rotorua, coming home every month or so to see my family, and it was on one of those visits about eight or nine months after Des's death that my brother Nathan told me a strange story.

Nathan still slept in the bedroom we had shared at the front of the house nearest the street. Early on the Saturday morning a week earlier he was woken from his sleep by the sound of someone whistling.

'It was definitely Des's whistle,' he said to me. 'After all those years I know that sound.'

I had to agree it was a distinctive sound, and we'd heard it every week since we were little.

'I heard the whistle and I thought I was dreaming. Then I heard the dogs. I got up and went to the window. A whole bunch of dogs were going up the road. Ours and every other mutt in town that was tied up was barking.'

I was a bit dubious about this, but Nathan assured me that others had heard it too. Later I asked Dad about it. He nodded.

'Yep. We all heard it. The dogs stayed away all day. They came home just like they used to when they went with Des. They were knackered.'

Great. Here was my family convinced that Des's ghost or something was taking the town's dogs out hunting. I really did think that I was being set up. But when I spoke to my mates who were still living at home, they said the same thing. One Saturday morning, just a week or so earlier, they had woken to the sound of the dogs. Some had even heard Des's whistle.

The next Friday night I was still at home. I bunked in my old bed and hardly slept. When dawn was approaching I got up, made a cup of tea and got back into bed, waiting. Nat woke up as well and we both just sat in our beds.

Nothing happened that Saturday morning, nor any other Saturday morning after that. It's been 10 years since Des died.

We've often talked about it but no one has any answers. The general opinion is that perhaps Des's spirit was hunting for his pigs. Or maybe he just wanted one last hunt before he went wherever spirits go. Whatever, half the town heard Des's whistle and the dogs definitely went bush that day.

The Old House

Now you see it, now you don't ... This story has been told to me by two different people on different occasions. Neither of the people concerned knows the other. In essence, what happened was virtually the same for both of them, although in each case the location and timing were quite different. The accounts differ only in minor details, but in the story I'm going to relate, the person involved went back years later to see if the experience repeated itself.

I was visiting whanau down on the East Coast in the early 1970s. Although I was born in the Gisborne area, I have lived most of my life in Auckland.

The occasion for the visit was the 100th birthday of my grandmother. Family had gathered from all over New Zealand and some even from Australia. The celebrations took place at Queen's Birthday Weekend, which was quite appropriate because Grandmother was a queen to all who knew her.

The celebration wasn't confined just to family – it involved our iwi and other neighbouring tribes. Grandmother had great mana among all the people on the coast.

The local marae was the site of most of the celebrations, and over several days Grandmother held centre stage, greeting friends and family from far and wide.

Because I hadn't been home since I was a child, I took the opportunity to slip away and explore the area whenever I could. One place that I wanted to see was where Grandmother and my mother had both been born, and where I spent my first three or four years.

I had faint memories of the place. I remembered the stream that ran beside the shingle road, and a small paddock surrounded by bush. There was one main house, with a wide verandah at the front. Behind were various sheds and whares.

Back then there were probably about 10 or 12 whanau living there. There was no electricity; the lighting was kerosene lantern or candles. Grandmother and Mum cooked on a wood and coal stove. Water for clothes washing and for bathing was heated up in the wash-house in a great big copper.

It was primitive by today's standards, I guess, but quite normal back then, and not just for Maori people. Everyone who lived in the country and didn't have the power on lived the same way. Some still do.

THE OLD HOUSE

It was on the Sunday evening that I decided to go and have a look for what had essentially been my first home. The light was fading when I left the marae and drove in the general direction of where I knew the place to be. I had asked my cousin Paul for directions and he had told me which turnoffs to take.

'Nothing to see now, bro,' he had said. 'Just a chimney and grass. The old people moved out years ago and there was a fire.'

But that didn't stop me. It was a memory and that was what the whole celebration was about – the memories of a wise old lady and, for me, the memories of my childhood, which were getting more and more hazy as time went on.

Even in the failing light I recognised the crossroads where Mum and Grandmother used to get off the bus with us kids, back from a visit to Gisborne. The roads had all been shingle then; now the main road was sealed, although the side road that led into the forest was still coarse gravel. Mum and Grandmother would carry or wheel my cousin, my sister and myself the five kilometres along the road to home.

I can remember their voices as they laughed and talked, and the sound of the creek that ran along the side of the road. I can still hear the sound of feet and carriage wheels on the shingle.

It was quite dark under the trees so I turned the headlights on full. It was obvious that no one really used the road much any more. In parts the gravel was mounded high enough to scrape the sump of my Mazda; in other places it was gone – replaced by clay, or a yawning pothole. In some places the creek had cut into the sides of the road and taken chunks away.

I drove very carefully, concentrating on the road. About a kilometre further up the road there was a sound of a big engine and a 4WD truck with more lights than a Christmas tree came roaring up behind me. Fortunately the road was wider at that point and I pulled over as far as I could as the big Toyota roared on past in a shower of stones. The driver honked once and was gone. I had a momentary glimpse of three faces in the front and some dogs on the back. Hunters, I thought. At least they still used the track.

I knew I was getting close to the old home site when I saw the big kauri stump. The tree was down before I was born, sawn down in the early days of European settlement of the area. The stump was three metres across: huge by any standards. Way back when, I can remember Dad lifting me up onto it to play.

Home was just around the corner. I realised the light was almost gone and I was disappointed. I had hoped I would have enough twilight left at least to get a bit of a look.

Paul had said it was just a chimney and lots of grass and weeds, so imagine my surprise when I turned the corner and saw my old home sitting there, lit up by the yellow glow of kerosene lanterns.

I turned off the engine and sat there, watching and listening. I could see shadows moving past the windows. There were voices laughing, talking. There was a guitar playing. I could hear children's voices.

Paul had obviously made a mistake – the old place was still in use. I decided that the guys in the Toyota must have been using it for a hunting camp and must have brought their families with them. I couldn't see the truck, but it could have been behind the house.

The front door opened and in the yellow light I could make out the dark shape of an old man as he stepped out onto the porch. He was hunched over and walked with a stick. The door closed and he walked across in front of a window, then sat down in a chair or couch. His head was clearly outlined by the light from the window behind him.

I had an urge to get out of the car and go up and greet him: introduce myself and find out who he was. I thought perhaps he was a distant relative visiting with his family for Grandmother's birthday. I didn't recognise him but there were a lot of old people I didn't know at the marae.

I had just started to get out of the car when I heard the sound of another big engine. I was sitting in the middle of the road, and the gateway into the yard of the old house was further on. I started the car and drove up, only to realise that the gateway had a huge ditch across it where a culvert pipe had obviously collapsed. I would have buried the nose of the car and done some serious damage if I'd carried on.

But the road was very narrow so I had to drive on and find a place where I could pull over and let the truck pass, then turn around. I could see the lights of the other vehicle on the trees ahead of me. It was coming up behind me pretty fast. Funny how guys with four-wheel drives always go so fast the moment they get off the tarseal.

I had to drive on quite a way but eventually I found a shoulder and squeezed over. This big tank didn't slow down and didn't honk. It was a yellow Land Cruiser and, like the other one, it was covered in lights, had dogs on the back and a crowd of men in the front.

Once the Cruiser was gone I started off again, still looking for a place to turn around. If I'd been driving a four-wheel drive I would have had no problems – I could have just nosed off the road through the ditch and swung around, but that wasn't an option in the Mazda. I drove on, increasingly frustrated the further I moved away from the old house.

Eventually I came to an intersection in the bush, perhaps four or five kilometres past the house site. The signpost pointing to the right said Kumita 8km. It was getting late and I'd lost the urge to go back the way I had come. I decided I would just head back to where I was staying and come back in the daylight before I went back to Auckland.

The birthday celebrations ran on until Tuesday. I had committed myself to being back at work on Thursday. My plan was that I would drive back Wednesday, after I had been back to the old house. I didn't catch up with Paul again until late on Tuesday, when we met for a quick farewell beer.

'I thought you told me the old place had burned down?' I said.

Paul looked at me with a puzzled expression on his face. 'Yeah – must be 15 years ago. Nothing left but the chimney and the remains of the old whares and sheds, but they're rotted just about flat.'

'I saw the place on Sunday night. People there, lights going. It was standing.' I replied.

Paul just laughed. 'You got the wrong place. A lot of the roads around here are confusing. You must have seen another outfit, eh.'

I was not convinced. I knew I'd got the right place.

Next morning I said my goodbyes and drove out south on the main road until I saw the turnoff. I had been right enough about the road I'd driven up on Sunday. I suppose I started to doubt myself a little when the big kauri stump wasn't around the next corner, or the next ... But then there it was. I think I breathed a big sigh of relief: I wasn't going mad after all.

I could see the green from the clearing through the trees as I got closer. I drove out of the shadows into bright sunlight and looked over towards the old house. It was gone.

I stood on the brakes hard enough to cause the car to skid. When I came to a stop I just sat there for a full minute without moving. The house was gone. All that remained was a stone fireplace with a metal flue at the top, nothing else – no porch, no sheds, nothing but weeds. The grass was tall, there were blackberries growing through it, and there was gorse. I could see one wall and some rusting tin off the whare I used to sleep in, but that was it.

Slowly I got out of the car and walked up the road to where the gate used to be. That at least was the way it had been three nights previously – with a big ditch between the old rotting gate posts. But the fence was gone; there were a few strands of rusty barbed wire left and the remains of a few posts.

I jumped over the ditch. An animal track led through the grass and brambles to where the front of the house had been. There was nothing there, just more brambles and the chimney and some elderberry bushes.

I stayed 10 minutes, then I heard a vehicle coming and went back to my car. I didn't bother trying to find a place to pull over, or get my camera out. There was no point. I just started the Mazda and drove away.

I don't know what happened that Sunday night, all I know is that it happened. I had the right place, no doubt about that. As to the time – I was perhaps 15 or 20 years early, or late, depending on which way you look at it.

When Grandmother died two years later I came down for her tangi. I went back to the old home site late one night by myself. There were no lights and no sounds except for the stream and a possum hissing in the trees. Whatever magic had taken place that Sunday night didn't come again for me.

I often wonder what would have happened if I had gone up to the old man on the porch and talked to him. What would he have said to me?

Rest in Peace

Mark was a member of a forestry team working in the central North Island when this incident occurred a few years ago. He's a pragmatic, practical, no-nonsense sort of guy who has worked in the bush since his 16th birthday.

We were doing some selective logging on a big bush terrace, taking out the prime trees and leaving the rest. It was a simple procedure. The guys who were spotting had been through the area and marked the trees to be felled with spray marker. The rest of us worked our way after them, dropping the marked ones.

We had a big Cat clearing runs for the skidder and dragging the felled trees down to where the skidder could get them and take them down to the stockpile area and the trucks for the mill.

There had been no dramas in the weeks we'd been at work in the block. The odd sailer (flying branch) had caused a bit of a scare now and again, and one of the boys had tried to remove his foot when a saw kicked back – the usual sort of thing. Logging is a dangerous game if you don't keep your eyes open and your mind on the job.

As we worked, the bush was filled with the sounds of our intrusion. The spluttering roar and whine of the chainsaws, the thud of the big diesels on the dozer and skidder, the squealing of the metal tracks on the Cat, the sound of the forest giants dying as they came crashing down.

I was working a saw, bringing down a big rimu. It was a few minutes to lunchtime. That was the magic time – and not just for the break and the tucker. I always looked forward to the silence that came with it. The racket we made was incredible – it was part of the job but I hated it. Still, no one has ever invented a silent chainsaw.

When smoko came and everything was shut down for a half hour the sounds of the bush came back. It was really peaceful.

We had an older guy on the dozer – a cantankerous old bloke called Rory. He was a good driver though. Rory was cutting a branch run for the skidder as smoko approached. I could just see him above me. He had the blade down and was taking off the lumps and bumps.

I concentrated on dropping my tree and then it was noon. I flicked off the saw, dropped it and my hard hat and started down to where the ute was parked. The other saws all fell silent as well, but Rory was still working. His was the only watch that told the right time in our gang. We were used to it. It generally got us an extra five minutes at smoko so we didn't complain. Not until knock-off, that is.

We had a few log chairs chainsawed out and a big stump as a table. It was a right little picnic spot. The other guys were already there when I got my bag out of the truck and sat down. Lunch for me was almost always the same but I didn't mind. I had a thermos of sweet black tea and Diane had made me three doorstop sandwiches: toast bread, heaps of butter, sliced mutton, relish and cheese. Bush tucker and I was into it. Then there was time for a leisurely mug of tea before it was back up the hill to sharpen the saw, trim out the tree I'd dropped and go on to the next.

'That old bugger loves the sound of his dozer almost as much as his own voice.' It was Jerry who first pointed out that Rory was over time, even for him. I had finished my first sandwich and was halfway through the next.

The dozer carried on and I must admit that it was pretty annoying. We all liked the silence at switch-off. It gave our ears and our heads a rest.

'Someone want to go up and tell him?' asked Joe, our foreman. None of us fancied the job so we just carried on eating.

For 10 minutes, seven of the eight-man crew sat at their lunch wishing for a silence that never came. They could hear the rumble of the bulldozer 100 yards away. They couldn't see it because of a small ridge and the bush. Eventually one of them noticed that the engine note didn't sound right.

'Something's wrong with the Cat,' said Greg. When I really listened I could also hear that something wasn't right.

'Might have caught a sailer,' one of the others suggested. But I'd been nearest to him and I knew that when I'd dropped my last tree Rory had been well clear.

We waited another minute, then Joe got to his feet. As boss, he had to check it out. A couple of us started off up the new track Rory had been carving.

As we climbed the Cat's diesel sounded like it was labouring heavily, pushing a big load, but the engine note didn't change. There was no let-off and no track sound. Something was very wrong. Joe started to run and we followed at a gallop. The rest of the guys had decided to come as well and they followed behind.

When we had scrambled up the final incline we saw that the big yellow bulldozer was sitting in a small clearing, its blade down, filled with soil and debris. The tracks weren't moving but blue diesel smoke filled the air, pumped from the exhaust. Rory was sitting bolt upright, totally motionless, each hand gripping a steering clutch.

We didn't know what to make of it. Some of the guys started shouting at Rory as we ran across to the Cat. He didn't seem to be injured, he was just sitting there.

'Heart attack?' someone shouted.

'Got no bloody heart,' someone else muttered.

We could see that the dozer was in drive, so why hadn't it blown up or stalled? Joe climbed gingerly up onto the tracks, scared they might start spinning and drag him under. They didn't move. He got on the running board and ducked into the cage.

'It's in gear!' he yelled, pushed the selector into neutral and knocked the throttle back. The engine noise immediately dropped to an idle. He hit the cut-off switch and the noise died right away.

Joe then turned his attention to Rory. There was no movement or sound from him, even though his eyes were wide open. Joe gave him a slap on the cheek. Not hard, but hard enough. Still no response.

'Give us a hand,' Joe called. A couple of us climbed up.

'We'll get him down then check him over,' said Joe. So we tried, but the old man's hands were damn near welded to the steering gear. We really had to prise them off. We did eventually, but we didn't want to break his fingers.

The three of us got him out of the cab and the others grabbed him and lowered him down. No sooner had he touched the ground than Rory woke up.

'What's going on?' he wanted to know.

'That's what we want to know,' said Joe. 'What happened?'

Rory stood up and shook his head. 'Damned if I know. Everything just stopped. I couldn't move. I was awake, I just couldn't move.'

'How are you feeling now?'

'Okay. Fine. I was just about to knock off for lunch. Thought I'd just do this last scrape, then everything just stopped and I couldn't move. I mean, I was in low gear. That amount of dirt wouldn't even lose me revs.'

'Might be an old kauri stump under there?' Curly suggested, nodding at the blade.

'That would've spun the tracks but it didn't. Just stopped moving.'

'Back it off and we'll see,' Joe suggested.

'I'll do it,' I said and jumped up into the cab. I switched on the ignition and hit the starter. The Cat was hot and the engine kicked into life immediately. I set the throttle, put the selector in reverse and let out the clutch. The engine note immediately changed. It started to labour again but the Cat didn't move. I played with the clutch and tried again. No go.

'Get the blade up!' Joe yelled. I tried, but the hydraulics wouldn't work.

Joe climbed up to have a go and I jumped down. Nothing worked except the engine. Eventually Joe gave up too.

'Can't happen like this – busting the transmission is one thing, but losing the hydraulics at the same time, no way.'

'We'll get the skidder up here and drag her back,' suggested Joe. 'Let's finish our lunch, then we'll have a go.'

We went back down to the ute and finished our tucker. Then Joe drove down to the log dump to the skidder. Now skidders are powerful machines. Basically they are huge tractor units, a bit like the driving unit of an earth scraper. Like the scrapers, they have enormous tyres rather than tracks. The big skidders can drag tons of logs behind them at a go.

Noddy the driver came roaring up the track and he manoeuvred so he could back up to the dozer. We hooked up a couple of heavy snig chains, Rory checked that the Cat was in neutral, then Joe gave Noddy the thumbs up. The skidder roared, the big tyres gripped and the Cat moved backwards as easily as you like. Noddy shut down and Rory climbed back onto the dozer.

He fired the Cat up and the first thing he did was raise the blade. No problem. He then selected reverse and backed up a bit. Easy. He pulled a clutch, kicked left away from where he had been stuck and drove 20 feet before backing up.

'Nothing wrong with her,' he said as he switched off. 'I'll give her a check over anyway, but as far as I can tell, she's fine.'

It was as we were standing, wondering what on earth was going on, that Curly went over to the mound of earth that the blade had been pushing when Rory had been stopped.

'Hey, you guys, come and have a look at this.'

We all trooped over to where he was standing.

I remember how the bones gleamed white and yellow against the black bush dirt. There was a skull and other bones I recognised as definitely human. There was some sort of cloth and there was a mere carved from greenstone. Curly was almost a full-blooded Maori and several of the others were part Maori. The significance of what we had found was more immediately obvious to them but we all soon got the message.

'An old warrior's grave probably. He was buried with honour – see his cloak and mere?' said Curly. 'It was a tapu that stopped you, Rory. This place is sacred.'

'What do we do now?' Joe asked. Like me, he was a Pakeha and stuff like this was a bit outside our experience.

'We'll get the tohunga and the elders to come and put it right,' said Curly, as if it were the most natural thing in the world. 'We'll just leave this place as it is, okay?'

'Not a problem,' said Joe.

So we went back to work. We finished that skidder run by putting a bend in it that took it away from that particular spot. Next day, and on company time and company pay, Curly brought some of his people up.

They had a ceremony at the grave site. The bones were reburied and we worked on around that place. We never had any more problems and I never experienced anything like that ever again in my 40-odd years in the bush.

Fire on the River

This incident took place in the mid-1970s on an isolated road that linked the East Coast with the central areas of the North Island. The road ran through large areas of native bush, at times parallel to a major river. In the small hours of one morning a group of young men were returning from the coast.

The five of us had been away over the East Coast for the weekend. It was my brother's 21st and it had been a great party. On Sunday we had a barbecue at the beach, went swimming and played rugby in the sand.

Afterwards it was back to Mum and Dad's for dinner, then we sat yarning until far too late. It was tough having to head home but we all had to work the next day.

Reid was driving with Marty next to him in the front. Jas, Willy and I were in the back. Willy was in the middle – sound asleep as usual. He could sleep anywhere. It was my car but we all took turns driving.

'Comfort stop!' called Jas at one stage.

'I'll stop up at the point,' replied Reid. The point was maybe half a mile ahead. It was the only place you could actually get off the road in about a five-mile stretch through the forest.

The bend was 50 feet ahead when Reid pulled over to the right and aimed towards the wide grassy verge. The left side was just clay bank and ditch.

The spot we stopped at looked down to the river below as it curved through the bush in a broad sweep.

I woke Willy and we all got out, wandering off to do what we had to do. The moon was peeping down at us through a window in the low cloud. There was a bit of mist around as always up there, but the rain that had come on in the evening had stopped for the moment.

I could see the river below us. It glistened black in the moonlight, looking like a thick gleaming snake through the matt black of the forest.

I'd stopped at this spot many times over the years. Dad used to take a break here on a long trip when we were kids and we would sometimes even have a picnic lunch.

But it's weird: I'd never really felt comfortable at that spot, even before that night. I'd driven past with a couple of Maori mates a few months

FIRE ON THE RIVER

before, on our way to play rugby on the coast. I'd wanted to stop for the usual but the others wouldn't.

'Bad place,' one of them said. 'We'll stop down the road a bit.' He never explained what was 'bad' about it, even though I asked.

That night as I stood there I felt a shiver run down my spine. It was nothing to do with the cold, and I don't think I imagined it.

'What's going on down there?' Marty suddenly called. 'Some mad buggers are having a barbie or something!'

I looked in the direction of his gaze and saw the faint flickering of fires on the far side of the bend in the river. Reid came over to where we stood.

There were five fires close to the water on the shingle of the shallow side of the bend, dim sparks of yellow and red crackling into the air.

'Three in the morning on a night like this and they're having a cook-up!' Reid laughed. 'Crazy!' he muttered, and started back for the car.

Jas and Willy came over to see what was going on.

'Listen! They're singing,' said Marty. We all shut up to listen. He was right.

'Chanting, more like,' said Jas. 'Some bunch of crazy Maoris having a hangi in the middle of the night!'

'Eerie sound, eh?' said Reid, who had given up on getting us back in the car for the moment and come back to stand with us.

'There's no road down there. They must have come in by boat.'

The very faint breeze must have changed because we could suddenly hear them more clearly. There was no other traffic on the road. Things were dead quiet but for what was coming up from below.

Suddenly another sound rose above the chanting. It was the sound of someone screaming. It was a high-pitched sound – I couldn't tell whether it was male or female. The scream ended abruptly and was followed by the sound of laughter.

'Oh brother,' said Willy. I've never seen faces glow pale in the night before, but ours did. Someone down there was in big trouble.

'Let's go. We'll phone the cops.' Reid was heading back for the car again.

Marty, Jas, Willy and I still stood staring down at the fires, which now flared more brightly. I squinted and I thought I could make out shapes moving beside them.

It was at that moment that the moon broke through again and we could see the pencil-thin shapes of boats protruding across the silver black of the water below. There were five or six of them. Long, black and sleek, bows to the bank, they pushed out into the water like fingers.

'Boats!' Marty whispered. 'Canoes. That's how they got there.'
'Pretty big canoes,' said Willy. '*Very* big canoes.'
'Let's get out of here, guys.' Reid wasn't keen to see any more. 'We'll call the cops when we get to town. There's nothing we can do.'
'Come on,' I agreed.
There were more screams from below, more laughter. I started to feel sick to my stomach.
'We're out of here.' I shoved Reid across into the passenger seat – I was a faster driver than he was. He didn't argue. The others scrambled in and I sent us bouncing back onto the road and took off.
Normally Reid would have been at me to slow down but he didn't say a word. We were all silent, trying not to think about what might have been happening back in the bush.
We got back to town just as dawn was breaking.
'We'll phone the cops from my place,' I told the others. My house was closest.
When we got inside, Cory, one of my flatmates, was already up. Cory is Maori, born and bred in the area. We'd been sharing the place for almost two years.
He could see we were pretty upset and asked what was up. Had we been in an accident or something?
I gabbled out the story as I went for the phone in the hall. Cory followed me, listening intently. Just as I was about to dial the police he reached out and cut me off.
'No cops, Paul. The crimes that were committed there happened a long time ago,' he said.
'What do you mean?' I asked. The other guys were in the kitchen doorway. Cory reluctantly led us back in there. The jug was boiling.
'Old-time stuff.' Cory was obviously uncomfortable talking about it, but we leaned on him as we made much-needed coffees and sat around the table. He knew he had to come clean.
'It's like this,' he said eventually. 'Years before the Pakeha arrived the tribes around here were fighting the tribes on the coast. Raiding parties travelled up and down the river like we use the road. Anyway, one time we were attacked and some of our people were taken away as slaves. The attackers stopped their journey at that big bend on the river. They camped there and killed some of their prisoners and ate them before they moved on. That place is tapu. No one goes there. You must have heard the spirits.'
That was all Cory would say on the matter. We didn't phone the police

in the end. I never stopped at that place again, no matter what. I had never believed in ghosts until then. Now I know they exist and it doesn't thrill me one little bit.

Poker Hand

The man who told me this tale thought it might be too 'far out' for inclusion in this collection. He swears the story is true, and that the inhabitants of a certain small East Coast town will verify it. It happened only a few years ago.

Card playing is one of those binge-type things people do, especially when the weather is bad, there's nothing on the telly, or you have the urge to have a bit of a gamble. That's the way I looked at it anyway, and so did a few of the others in town.

It was midwinter, raining like crazy, and there was no outside work other than for the road gangs who were busy clearing slips. Quite a few of us were in forestry so there was nothing for us to do while the weather was so bad.

Someone (probably me) thought it was time that the card school came out of hibernation. We had a big game about once every six months. There were smaller ones going all the time but this was 'the school', and the whole district was in on it.

Word quickly got around and we did what we normally did, which was use the back room down at the hall.

At the appointed time of seven o'clock on Friday night we got the old pot-belly stove glowing red hot, moved in some beers and a few bottles of coke. A couple of the women were jacked up to organise the kai and we were into it.

The game was poker – straight stud, take no prisoners. No cash up and leave, this was last one standing (or sitting): winner takes all. We had six chairs and as one fell out, there was always someone to step in.

The spectators were four deep around the table.

We played all through Friday night and four of the seats had changed a couple of times. I was still in and sitting pretty, and so was my mate George. There was a lot of money up. We used chips, but the banker in charge was a non-player.

Old Pete was the man. He sat at a small table to one side and issued chips when required. He had two shoeboxes: one for chips, the other full of money – and I mean full. Thursday had been payday at the works up the road, and for the forestry boys.

At the end of the game old Pete got 10 per cent of the pot. That was fair, because he was also the arbitrator in any dispute, and his son Darby was the man who made sure that order was kept.

Darby was a brisket-puncher at the works and he was built like the entire All Black front row rolled into one. He was gentle and quiet, but no one ever argued with him.

We stopped every four hours or so for a break, to stretch our legs, have a bite. Typically, we played until we dropped and if you went to sleep, you forfeited.

I'd won a few over the years. You sure earned your money, especially when the game went on for the best part of a week, which it sometimes did. I've won with only $100 in chips against thousands. The other guy needed sleep so badly that in the end he just stumbled off to his bed, leaving me the winner. It was pretty brutal but we were all big boys, we knew what we were in for.

We played right through to midday Saturday and then we were allowed an hour off. It wasn't enough time for a sleep but it was a chance to grab some fresh air and a sit-down meal. Except that most of us actually stood to eat in order to give our bums a rest. I had my own cushion, but even then the old behind got sore.

'Who's going to be a stayer?' George asked me as we walked around the hall. It was still raining outside.

'All of them,' I said. The team that were at the table now were old hands. Unless someone could clean house, we could conceivably still be playing on Monday.

We settled into it again, the ranks of spectators rising and falling throughout the rest of the day. The All Blacks were playing Australia in the Bledisloe Cup that weekend so things were pretty thin about eight on Saturday night.

One of the floating chairs had just tossed his hand in when at that moment a man none of us had ever seen before came in. He just walked in the door and straight to the empty seat. There were others waiting but they all just stood there. No one complained because this guy was very weird looking.

The stranger was like some character out of a western. He was Maori, sure, well – what we could see of him looked Maori. He wore a leather cowboy-style hat and a big black leather coat, one of those long ones right down to the ground. The collar of the coat was half up. His nose was long and thin, his eyes dark, his moustache black and drooping at the corners, and he had a wide mouth with plenty of white teeth.

'Kia ora,' he said in a very deep voice. We all greeted him. He turned to Pete at the side table and handed him five new $100 notes. Pete gave him chips. I noticed that his hands and the fingers were very dark and very long. There were no names offered.

Play started again, and the stranger spoke only when necessary. By the time we stopped for our midnight break it was obvious that the newcomer was winning big time. I was getting down on chips, so was George, and the other chairs had changed, one of them a couple of times.

While the rest of us went to the toilet and wandered around having some kai, the stranger just sat at the table, his hands flat on the table in front of him, waiting. Some of the spectators tried to talk to him, to find out where he came from.

'Around,' was all he said, and he just smiled.

Well, we never made it to the next break. The stranger just cleaned us right out. It was like he just couldn't lose a hand. He was betting 100 a time and winning virtually every hand.

I went out completely gutted, and George followed shortly afterwards. A couple of the floating chairs hung in there for a while, then it was all over.

Pete and Darby collected all the chips, Pete counted the money, and believe me, it was a decent amount. Pete then counted out his 10 per cent, while the stranger just sat watching, with his eyes half hidden under the brim of his hat and this wide grin on his face.

He took the big stack of money that Pete handed him, and as he stood, he pushed it into a pocket in his long coat.

'A pleasure, gentlemen,' he said in that deep, deep voice.

We realised then just how tall he was – maybe six foot four or five.

'Kia ora,' we said, and he was just going out the door when the hem of his coat flicked in the wind. I was one of about 10 people whose eyes were drawn to his feet.

I guess with the rest of his get-up, we had expected some ornate cowboy boots. But in those few seconds as he stepped out the door we all gaped at what we saw instead: cloven hooves.

We just stood there, the door closed and there was total silence. We stood blinking, open mouthed. Then George leapt at the door and pulled it open. We all ran outside. The carpark was empty but for our cars and trucks. No strange vehicles, no stranger. In a matter of seconds he had gone.

A couple of us ran to the corner of the building so we could see across the football field towards the bush. Even on this stormy night there was enough moonlight to see that there was no one there. He would have had to be an Olympic sprinter to get across in the time it took for us to get to the corner of the hall.

We all went back inside and stood around the stove. We were a tired and pretty confused bunch, I can tell you.

'Turehu,' said old Pete finally. 'He was a Turehu. He came among us to play one of their tricks on us.'

The Turehu are a fairy people from Maori mythology, who dwell in the forests of the North Island. In the south there is a different fairy 'tribe' called the Maero Ero.

To all intents and purposes the Turehu resemble humans, but there is one notable difference: cloven hooves. They are not satanic, as you might think if you are of European heritage. The Turehu are the Children of the Mist of Maori mythology. Like the leprechauns of Ireland they are often mischievous, given to playing tricks on their human neighbours.

The Maero Ero of the South Island, while quite different in physical appearance to the Turehu, with hair-covered bodies and fewer human features, have the same sense of mischief.

Everyone in this town is convinced that our card game was won by a Turehu. But what we are all wondering is what did he want with all that money?

'To go to the casino in Auckland!' someone suggested. 'They'll never notice him as being any different from their usual customers!'

Some of the others are hoping the card-playing Turehu might come back for the next big game so they can have a go at getting their money back.

PUBLISHER'S NOTE

Maybe you have a story about something you can't explain? We invite you to write in to Shoal Bay Press at Box 17-661, Christchurch, with a brief outline of your experience and we will pass it on to the editors for possible inclusion in a new collection of *Tales of the Supernatural in Aotearoa*. Please include your name and contact details.